"This groundbreaking book offers a masterful synthesis of coaching strategies and corporate innovation, with a keen focus on the human elements that drive successful collaborations. The authors' systematic approach to bridging cultural gaps and fostering trust between corporations and startups is both practical and insightful. Their emphasis on character-based leadership and the 'people before technology' principle provides a fresh perspective that's essential for today's innovation landscape. An invaluable resource for corporate leaders, coaches, and anyone involved in open innovation initiatives."

Nelson Yip, *Hong Kong SAR Government The Medal of Honor Recipient, Torch Bearer and Paralympian, Beijing 2008 Olympics, Honorary Fellow, The City University of Hong Kong & Lingnan University of Hong Kong*

"This book offers coaches working with clients in this fast-paced corporate world a clearly signposted systemic approach to coaching for corporate innovation that is rooted in the authors' extensive knowledge and experience of corporate leaders as well as organisational strategy and leadership in the corporate world. Beyond offering specific steps, it helps the coach understand the challenges at every turn in context and from the perspective of their clients. The book is a treasure trove for reflective practitioners who want to understand their clients within their unique systems and build on the leadership knowledge, theory and research brought together in this book."

Silvia King, *Positivity International, EMCC Global Research Accelerator co-lead*

"In today's fast-moving business landscape, 'Coaching Strategies for Corporate Innovation' delivers exactly what organizations need – a practical roadmap for bridging the gap between corporate stability and startup agility. Ivan Yong Wei Kit and Sam Lee have created something special here, drawing from their wealth of experience to show how coaching transforms innovation partnerships.

What impressed me most was their insight that innovation success isn't primarily about technology, but about people, culture and leadership character. Their three-phase approach – Matching Innovation, Collaborative Innovation, and Ecosystem Innovation – tackles the human challenges that often derail corporate-startup collaborations.

The book shines with real-world case studies that bring these concepts to life. Whether you're an innovation leader, coach, or entrepreneur, you'll find immediately applicable strategies for building trust, aligning vision, and creating sustainable partnerships.

This is essential reading for anyone serious about corporate innovation. The authors have delivered a work that's both intellectually stimulating and practically valuable – a rare combination that makes this book a must-have resource."

Lim Chee Gay, *Managing Director – GOC APAC, The Access Group*

"This book is an essential contribution to corporate innovation and growth, highlighting the concept of intrapreneurship . It is accessible, clearly written, and explores the often overlooked area of coaching in corporate innovation. The authors effectively connect coaching with corporate innovation, emphasizing that successful innovation begins with people building trust and collaboration within and outside organizations. Successive chapters convincingly argue for the role of coaching in corporate innovation and provide guidance on phases of innovation and impactful coaching areas. A brilliant read for coaches and corporate leaders."

Alison Mitchell, *EMCC Global Head of Centre for Excellence in Research*

"This insightful book co-authored by Ivan Yong Wei Kit and Sam Lee expertly combines theoretical frameworks with practical coaching methodologies, offering a comprehensive systemic approach to fostering corporate innovation through collaborating with startup companies. The authors present coaching not merely as an adjunctive practice but as a transformative power in corporate innovation, an essential catalyst for stakeholders' alignment. Acknowledging the volatility and continuous transformation of today's business environment, they focus on trust-building through application of emotional intelligence, coachability, co-creation, and transparency, providing indispensable guidance for cultivating sustainable corporate innovation ecosystems."

Andrey Kostyuk, *CEO, Founder @ AAlchemy Ventures | Angel Investor and EMCC-accredited Startup Mentor*

Coaching Strategies for Corporate Innovation

Drawing upon the authors' own extensive experiences within the field, and melding startup dynamics with corporate innovation, the book equips readers to navigate the complexities of this emerging innovation practice.

Collaboration between large corporations and innovative startups represents a strategic pillar of corporate innovation and is growing at a rapid pace globally. Such engagements are situated within the broader paradigm of open innovation and are categorised explicitly as corporate venturing when they involve mechanisms such as strategic investments, partnerships, incubators, or co-development initiatives. Leveraging the authors' extensive experience in startup investment, mentorship, and corporate innovation thought leadership forums, this book addresses the critical need for innovation coaching strategies to succeed in this dynamic corporate-startup collaboration. Through a synergy of practical insights, riveting case studies, and authoritative thought leadership, readers will be guided on a transformative journey encompassing innovation culture, symbiotic partnerships with startups, and the coaching strategies pivotal for unlocking innovation advantage.

This book is tailored for corporate leaders, innovation teams, corporate venture capitalists, and professional coaches aspiring to transcend conventional wisdom in the current corporate innovation practices.

Ivan Yong Wei Kit is an organizational psychologist, engineer, author and a startup angel investor. In the startup space, Ivan mentors for MDEC (a Malaysian startup agency) and an Adjunct Professor in Entrepreneurship and Social Innovation with UNITAR. He also co-founded the Corporate Disruptors Forum, a leading international platform advocating corporate innovation and collaboration with startups. Ivan is an active member of the European Mentoring & Coaching Council (EMCC), where he is a Board member & co-President for the Asia Pacific Region, and the Head of Global Social Responsibilities Initiatives leading social responsibility programs in Africa, Asia and Europe. Ivan is the co-author of "Department of Startup: Why Every Fortune 500 Should Have One" and a contributing author in "The Ethical Coaches' Handbook. A Guide to Developing Ethical Maturity in Practice" (Routledge 2022).

Sam Lee is a serial entrepreneur and startup angel investor/mentor. He co-founded the Corporate Disruptors Forum, an international platform for accelerating the corporate innovation and entrepreneurship ecosystem. He is also a founding member of Innovative Business Foundation, a non-profit organization for charitable works to assist the development of young scientists and entrepreneurs in China and Hong Kong SAR. Sam co-authored "Department of Startup: Why Every Fortune 500 Should Have One" and was the producer/editor of the "Hong Kong Society of Economists Magazine," during his tenure.

The Professional Coaching Series

This series brings together leading exponents and researchers in the coaching field to provide a definitive set of core texts important to the development of the profession. It aims to meet two needs - a professional series that provides the core texts that are theoretically and experimentally grounded, and a practice series covering forms of coaching based in evidence. Together they provide a complementary framework to introduce, promote and enhance the development of the coaching profession.

Titles in the series:

The Evidence-Based Practitioner Coach: Understanding the Integrated Experiential Learning Process
By Lloyd Chapman

An Integral Approach to Transformative Leadership: Dancing Through the Storm
By Dorrian Aiken

A Guide to Formulation in Coaching
By David A. Lane, Sarah Corrie and Louise C. Kovács

Coaching Strategies for Corporate Innovation: A Systemic Approach to Coaching Teams and Leaders
Ivan Yong, Sam Lee

Internal Coaching: The Inside Story, 2nd Edition
By Katharine St John-Brooks and Julia Duncan

For further information about this series please visit https://www.routledge.com/The-Professional-Coaching-Series/book-series/KARNPROFC

Coaching Strategies for Corporate Innovation

A Systemic Approach to Coaching Teams and Leaders

Ivan Yong and Sam Lee

Routledge
Taylor & Francis Group

LONDON AND NEW YORK

Designed cover image: © Getty Images

First published 2025
by Routledge
4 Park Square, Milton Park, Abingdon, Oxon OX14 4RN

and by Routledge
605 Third Avenue, New York, NY 10158

Routledge is an imprint of the Taylor & Francis Group, an informa business

© 2025 Ivan Yong and Sam Lee

The right of Anuja Khanna to be identified as author of this work has been asserted in accordance with sections 77 and 78 of the Copyright, Designs and Patents Act 1988.

British Library Cataloguing-in-Publication Data
A catalogue record for this book is available from the British Library

Library of Congress Cataloging-in-Publication Data
A catalog record has been requested for this book

ISBN: 978-1-032-74419-3 (hbk)
ISBN: 978-1-032-74681-4 (pbk)
ISBN: 978-1-003-46915-5 (ebk)

DOI: 10.4324/9781003469155

Typeset in Times New Roman
by Taylor & Francis Books

Thanks be to God and Jesus Christ for the grace to pen this book, and to my wife, Nancy, for being the quiet force supporting my work. (Ivan Yong)

Contents

Series Foreword

A Vision for the Future of Coaching in a Volatile Corporate Environment

As the authors contend, the corporate environment has become increasingly volatile, and the strategies adopted in the past no longer meet the need of an era of disruption and relentless technological change. The answer they suggest is the path of corporate innovation, which itself is far from easy and is full of challenges for which past behavior may not provide the key.

Yet, if this is a difficult world for leaders to navigate, it increases the complexities that coaches face in assisting leaders to explore what change means as they seek to understand and act to not just survive but also thrive in this new landscape. Coaches will need to adapt, but first they have to seek to understand this environment and the issues leaders face. The authors set out in the first part of the book the nature of corporate innovation and why it matters. They provide valuable examples to guide the reader to what works or does not. Having provided that background, they then explore what this means for innovation in coaching. This section enables the reader to grasp the challenges faced by organizations and coaches working with them. The authors succeed in their aim to demystify the process of corporate innovation and set the groundwork for practical approaches that organizations as well as coaches can take to embrace change.

A notable feature of their approach is to establish each chapter as a guide in its own right so readers can make use of the ideas as they go along as well as build their understanding section by section. This enlightening balance of theory, examples, and practice will appeal to our readers of the Professional Coaching Series, who often want to see ideas explored, supported, and brought to life so that they can challenge their own thinking and apply their reflections to work with clients. However, it is not just coaches who will gain from this balance. Corporate leaders and innovators will find much in the book to help them explore the multitude of challenges that technology presents as well as the benefits it can bring if we focus on people as well as processes so that innovation augments the capabilities we will need to build a vison for the future.

In Part II, the authors build on the foundations to consider startup organizations as sources of innovation and the issues raised through selecting partnerships for collaboration. They make the essential point that selecting such partnerships is not just about the "the startup's technological offerings, business model, market potential, and alignment with corporate objectives"; it is also fundamentally about the founding team, the people, and the cultural fit between them and the corporates seeking to build innovation through engagement. They explore both successful and unsuccessful examples to assist both leaders and coaches. In addition, they provide clear guidance on ways to build success based on their own practice, research, and market studies. This approach to matching innovation among startups, partnering corporates, and coaches through understanding success and failure is a firm foundation for their subsequent consideration of the creation of shared visions and dreams.

It is often proclaimed that culture is key, and in the coaching world, this is a well-established principle of practice. Here the authors explore why it matters so much in creating collaboration for innovation. Ways to navigate it and the importance of building trust before collaboration lead into a discussion of the pillars for creating the positive dynamics necessary for establishing trust in the corporate environment.

The ecosystem of innovation is one of constant movement, and the need to pivot to different positions is a continuous process. This concept is engaged through the idea of progressive pivoting and the dynamics that this entails. Again, case studies are used to bring the theory to life in an example of successful corporate pivots. This section enables our readers to examine key takeaways for the book on the emergent role of corporate innovation, building the necessary relationships, the convergence of people and technologies, and the future of AI coaching.

The book concludes with a call to action.

The authors bring extensive experience of working with innovation, detailed case examples, clearly explored and relevant literature, and a wealth of coaching frameworks. Their knowledge of the field is used to provide the reader with both a guide and a way to innovate as a leader or coach. I can thoroughly recommend this book as a worthwhile contribution to the Professional Coaching Series and to anyone looking to understand the world of innovation.

David A. Lane
Professional Development Foundation

Preface

Authors' Background

This book reflects the combined expertise and transformative experiences of Ivan Yong Wei Kit and Sam Lee and their commitment to transforming corporate innovation with coaching strategies.

Ivan is a recognized authority in open innovation and leadership coaching, with a career dedicated to empowering organizations to embrace change and achieve lasting transformation. As a cofounder of the Corporate Disruptors Forum, Ivan has created a platform where corporate leaders, startup founders, and innovators converge to discuss, shape, and implement groundbreaking ideas. His leadership extends to Nanyang Angelz, an angel investment group that has nurtured numerous startups, bridging the gap between corporate ecosystems and entrepreneurial ventures. Ivan's insights into aligning corporate strategies with startup agility are encapsulated in his acclaimed book, coauthored with Sam Lee, *Department of Startup: Why Every Fortune 500 Should Have One.*

Sam Lee is an entrepreneur, angel investor, and mentor, guiding startup founders through the complexities of innovation and competitive markets. As an integral contributor to the Corporate Disruptors Forum, Sam has helped shape discussions that redefine disruptions and innovation. His role as a mentor and investor at Nanyang Angelz highlights his ability to identify and support high-potential startups, fostering collaboration between entrepreneurial and corporate entities.

Together, Ivan and Sam bring a unique blend of practical expertise and passion for bridging the worlds of corporations and startups. Their shared experiences in creating synergies between these domains make this book a vital resource for leaders, coaches, and innovators seeking to unlock the full potential of corporate innovation. Both authors share a belief in the transformative potential of collaboration, trust, and innovation, which forms the foundation of this work.

Why Is This Book Written?

The corporate landscape has become a battleground of disruption with increasing intensity over the years. In an era defined by volatile market dynamics and relentless technological advancement, the ability to innovate determines survival. Corporations can no longer rely on legacy strategies; they must actively seek partnerships, cultivate creativity, and embrace change. However, the road to successful innovation is fraught with challenges, stemming mainly from poor leadership, cultural clashes, misaligned goals, and a lack of trust.

This book is written with the conviction that corporate innovation holds the key to not only staying competitive but thriving in this new world. Coaching, as a discipline and practice, is the bridge that connects the complexities of corporate innovation to tangible, sustainable successes. Through deliberate coaching strategies, companies can align their resources, empower their people, and transform challenges into opportunities.

The Purpose and Objectives

This book serves a dual purpose. First, it seeks to demystify the intricate processes of corporate innovation, providing practical insights grounded in real-world applications. Second, it highlights the role of coaching as a pivotal enabler in navigating the complexities of corporate innovation.

Our primary audience includes human resources professionals, corporate innovation leaders, open innovation practitioners, coaches, and startup founders. We aim to equip these readers with a comprehensive understanding of coaching strategies tailored for corporate innovation. This book offers tools and frameworks that are not only applicable but essential for creating a thriving culture of collaboration and transformation.

How to Get the Most From This Book

This book is designed with both flexibility and depth. Each chapter functions as a standalone guide, offering actionable insights on specific aspects of corporate innovation and coaching. At the same time, the chapters build upon one another, forming a cohesive narrative that covers the entire spectrum of corporate innovation.

Readers can approach the book in a way that suits their immediate needs—whether it is gaining clarity on coaching techniques, understanding cultural integration, or mastering trust-building strategies. Collectively, the chapters provide a holistic view of how coaching serves as an indispensable bridge for the phases of corporate innovation.

A Vision for the Future

We stand at a critical juncture where technology, such as artificial intelligence (AI), cloud computing, Internet of Things (IOTs), blockchain technology, quantum computing, and human ingenuity, converge to shape the future of work and business. In this rapidly evolving landscape, the human element—character, vision, and emotional intelligence—becomes more significant than ever. Coaching, as a practice, addresses this need by focusing on people as much as processes, ensuring that technology serves to augment rather than replace human capabilities.

Our vision is to inspire corporate leaders and innovators to embrace coaching as a transformative tool, enabling them to navigate uncertainty, foster resilience, and unlock their full potential. As readers engage with this book, it is hoped that they will discover not only practical tools but also be inspired to lead with authenticity, humility, and courage.

Through its case studies, frameworks, and practical strategies, this book invites the readers to rethink the possibilities of corporate innovation and embark on a journey that combines technological advancement with the enduring power of human connection. The authors believe that coaching, as a bridge, can unlock unprecedented opportunities for innovation and transformation—redefining leadership and collaboration in disruptive times.

Acknowledgments

Coaching Strategies for Corporate Innovation: A Systemic Approach to Coaching Teams and Leaders is a result of a collaborative effort shaped by the insights, challenges, and contributions of numerous individuals and organizations dedicated to advancing corporate innovation.

This work has been enriched by the experiences of corporate innovators, startup founders, and professional coaches who have generously shared their journeys. Their perspectives have played a vital role in shaping the frameworks and strategies presented in this book.

The Corporate Disruptors Forum (CDF) and its collaborators and partners receive special recognition. Their commitment to corporate innovation, open innovation, and corporate–startup collaborations has provided essential insights that strengthen this work. The industry leaders driving progress in these fields continue to demonstrate the power of innovation when guided by strong leadership and strategic vision.

A special acknowledgment is extended to Zoe Lau Gungor, CDF's producer for forums and events, whose dedication to fostering meaningful discussions on innovation has been instrumental. Her work in bringing together thought leaders and innovation communities has helped shape the conversations that fuel progress in this space.

We would also like to acknowledge the following individuals who have been instrumental in shaping our work and for their unwavering support. Special thanks to:

Professor David Lane, for his belief that this book will bring significant contribution to the coaching world.

Professor Cecilia Chan, for being a role model and mentor, in the pursuit of transformative innovation backed by strong research.

Dr Eleftheria Egel, for her tireless partnership in research work.

Professor Anthony Teo, for his mentoring and inspiring work in business innovation.

Alison Mitchell, for her leadership in executing research projects with excellence.

Silvia King, for her strong support and the constant nudge to be courageous.

Gratitude is also owed to mentors and peers in leadership development, coaching, and corporate innovation. Their unwavering support, thought-provoking discussions, and critical feedback have contributed significantly to refining and strengthening the ideas in this book.

Appreciation is extended to the publishing team, editors, and reviewers, whose meticulous attention to detail and dedication to excellence have ensured that these strategies and frameworks reach those who will benefit most.

Finally, heartfelt thanks go to Nancy (Ivan's wife) and Sam's family, friends, and close colleagues who have offered patience, encouragement, and unwavering belief in this work. Their support has provided the foundation that made this book possible.

This book is dedicated to those leading innovation, driving transformation, and building collaborative ecosystems that shape the future of business. May it serve as a valuable resource in advancing their work and amplifying their impact.

Ivan Yong & Sam Lee

Part I

Introduction to Corporate Innovation and Coaching Innovation

Chapter 1

Corporate Innovation

The global business landscape is undergoing a seismic shift. Accelerated technological advancements, market transitions, and pervasive disruptions are reshaping industries at an unprecedented pace. Emerging technologies do not simply enhance existing business models; they redefine them entirely. The World Economic Forum's 2023 report identifies several key emerging technologies expected to significantly impact society and industries, including AI-driven biotech, next-generation batteries, and space-based solar power (World Economic Forum, 2023, p. 5). Companies can no longer rely on traditional strategies; they must innovate or risk obsolescence. This relentless pace of change demands a proactive approach, especially in a world increasingly focused on sustainability.

Sustainability has become more than just a buzzword; it is now an imperative for businesses. Growing awareness of environmental degradation, climate change, and resource scarcity compels companies to rethink their operations fundamentally. Ignoring the environmental and social impact of their actions is no longer an option. The shift toward sustainability is not only ethically necessary but also financially prudent. Businesses that fail to integrate sustainable practices into their core strategies may soon find themselves irrelevant in a rapidly evolving market (Christensen, 2016, p. 22).

Moreover, the volatile, uncertain, complex, and ambiguous (VUCA) economy amplifies the challenges faced by corporations. This environment, characterized by rapid changes and unpredictability, demands agility and resilience. Traditional approaches to competition and market relevance falter in the face of VUCA dynamics. To stay competitive, corporations must develop the ability to anticipate and respond to these changes with speed and precision (Reeves & Deimler, 2011, p. 135). Cultivating a culture of innovation throughout the organization is essential to navigate this landscape (Bennett & Lemoine, 2014, p. 27).

1.1 Importance of Corporate Innovation in the New Economy

Corporate innovation emerges as the antidote to these challenges. It offers a pathway for companies to not only survive but thrive in this turbulent environment. Innovation enables businesses to create new products, services, and

DOI: 10.4324/9781003469155-2

processes that meet evolving customer needs and adapt to market changes. It empowers companies to explore new business models, enter untapped markets, and differentiate themselves from competitors (Kiron et al., 2013, p. 71). According to Deloitte, companies that prioritized innovation were 2.6 times more likely to outperform their peers in financial metrics, highlighting innovation as a key differentiator in times of disruption (Deloitte, 2021, p. 15). Similarly, PwC found that 54% of global executives identified innovation as a top priority for growth and sustainability in their organisations (PwC, 2017, p. 9).

1.1.1 What Is Corporate Innovation?

Corporate innovation refers to the systematic efforts by established organizations to create new value through the development and implementation of new ideas, products, services, or business models. Unlike startups, which often build their entire existence around a single innovative idea, corporate innovation involves navigating within the complexities of large, established systems. It requires balancing the need for innovation with the operational demands of maintaining existing business functions.

Henry Chesbrough, a pioneer of the open innovation concept, explores corporate innovation in the context of collaboration in his book *Open Innovation: The New Imperative for Creating and Profiting from Technology*. He defines corporate innovation as the process by which companies engage with external partners—such as startups, universities, and even competitors—to innovate more effectively. Chesbrough argues that this approach allows companies to leverage external ideas and technologies, thereby accelerating innovation cycles and reducing costs (2003, p. 23).

In their book *Managing Innovation: Integrating Technological, Market, and Organizational Change,* Tidd and Bessant (2018) describe corporate innovation as a systematic process where large organizations introduce new ideas, processes, or products to sustain or improve their competitive position. They emphasize that innovation in corporate settings is not just about creating new products but involves integrating technological, market, and organizational changes to drive overall business success (p. 48).

O'Reilly and Tushman (2016), in *Lead and Disrupt: How to Solve the Innovator's Dilemma,* discuss the concept of corporate innovation as the ability of established companies to explore new opportunities while exploiting existing capabilities. This dual approach, known as ambidexterity, is crucial for corporations to innovate successfully. The authors argue that corporations must strike a balance between refining their current operations and venturing into new, innovative territories to remain competitive in a rapidly changing market (p. 22).

In *The Innovator's Solution: Creating and Sustaining Successful Growth,* Christensen and Raynor (2013) focus on corporate innovation as a means for established companies to identify and capitalize on disruptive innovations.

They argue that by understanding and anticipating disruptive trends, corporations can sustain long-term growth and avoid being outpaced by more agile competitors. This perspective underscores the importance of proactive innovation strategies in maintaining a corporation's market position (p. 56).

The common thread across these definitions of corporate innovation highlights the critical role of collaboration, strategic adaptation, and organizational capability in driving innovation. Whether through leveraging external partnerships (Chesbrough), integrating technological and organisational changes (Tidd and Bessant), balancing exploration and exploitation (O'Reilly and Tushman), or navigating disruptive trends (Christensen and Raynor), corporate innovation is portrayed as a proactive and systematic approach. It underscores the importance of adaptable structures and forward-looking strategies, which are crucial for maintaining competitiveness and responding effectively to dynamic market challenges.

1.1.2 Trends in Corporate Innovation

In recent years, corporate innovation has evolved from being a buzzword to a critical strategic imperative. Several trends highlight the growing importance of innovation within corporate environments:

1 **Open Innovation**: Companies increasingly embrace open innovation, which involves collaborating with external partners such as startups, research institutions, and even competitors. This approach allows companies to tap into external knowledge, accelerate innovation cycles, and reduce costs. For example, Procter & Gamble's Connect + Develop program successfully leveraged open innovation to generate over 50 percent of its product innovations through external collaborations (Chesbrough, 2011, p. 56).

2 **Corporate Venturing**: Many corporations now invest in or acquire startups to foster innovation. These investments not only provide financial returns but also offer access to new technologies, talent, and business models. Google Ventures, the venture capital arm of Alphabet Inc., has invested in numerous startups that complement and enhance its core business, such as Uber, Slack, and Nest Labs (Gompers & Lerner, 2013, p. 89).

3 **Digital Transformation**: The advent of digital technologies has become a driving force for corporate innovation. Companies across industries are leveraging technologies like artificial intelligence, blockchain, and the Internet of Things (IoT) to innovate their products, services, and operations. For instance, General Electric (GE) underwent a significant digital transformation, investing heavily in its Predix platform to harness the power of IoT in industrial applications (Westerman et al., 2014, p. 132).

4 **Sustainability and Social Innovation**: Increasingly, companies are focusing on sustainability and social impact as part of their innovation strategies.

This trend aligns with the growing consumer and regulatory demand for environmentally and socially responsible business practices. Unilever's Sustainable Living Plan, which aims to decouple the company's growth from its environmental footprint while increasing its positive social impact, serves as a prominent example (Polman, 2016, p. 22).

1.2 Open Innovation: The Overarching Concept for Corporate Venturing, Digital Transformation, and Sustainability and Social Innovation

Open innovation serves as a broad framework that encompasses corporate venturing, digital transformation, and sustainability and social innovation. At its core, open innovation encourages companies to look beyond their internal resources and collaborate with external partners to drive innovation. This approach not only broadens the scope of available knowledge and technology but also accelerates the innovation process by tapping into external expertise.

Corporate venturing is a prime example of open innovation in action. By investing in and partnering with startups, corporations gain access to cutting-edge technologies, new talent, and innovative business models. These strategic alliances allow companies to integrate external innovations into their operations, which exemplifies the essence of open innovation—leveraging external resources to enhance internal capabilities (Chesbrough, 2011, p. 42).

Digital transformation, while often associated with the adoption of new technologies, is also deeply rooted in open innovation. Companies undergoing digital transformation frequently engage with external technology providers, startups, and research institutions to integrate advanced digital solutions into their business models. This collaboration with external partners reflects the principles of open innovation, as it involves sourcing external knowledge and technologies to drive internal digital initiatives (Westerman et al., 2014, p. 109).

Sustainability and social innovation further illustrate the comprehensive nature of open innovation. In these areas, companies collaborate with non-governmental organizations (NGOs), governments, and other stakeholders to address environmental and social challenges. These partnerships enable companies to align their innovation strategies with broader societal goals, drawing on external expertise and resources to create sustainable and socially impactful solutions. This collaborative effort underscores the open innovation framework, where external partnerships are essential for achieving meaningful outcomes (Polman, 2016, p. 27).

Open innovation is the overarching concept that includes corporate venturing, digital transformation, and sustainability and social innovation. Each of these strategies relies on external collaborations to drive innovation, demonstrating how open innovation serves as the foundation for diverse and impactful innovation initiatives.

1.2.1 Notable Case Studies in Corporate Innovation/Open Innovation

Several case studies illustrate the successful implementation of corporate innovation strategies:

1. **Apple Inc.**: Apple's relentless focus on innovation has positioned it as a leader in consumer electronics. The introduction of the iPhone in 2007 exemplified disruptive innovation, revolutionizing the mobile phone industry and setting new standards for user experience. Apple's innovation strategy emphasizes seamless integration of hardware, software, and services, creating an ecosystem that fosters customer loyalty (Yoffie & Rossano, 2018, p. 104).
2. **Tesla, Inc.**: Tesla's approach to innovation extends beyond its electric vehicles to its business model and manufacturing processes. The company's direct-to-consumer sales model, coupled with its over-the-air software updates, has disrupted the traditional automotive industry. Tesla's Gigafactories also exemplify innovation in large-scale manufacturing, aiming to produce batteries and electric vehicles more efficiently (Stringham et al., 2015, p. 67).
3. **Amazon.com, Inc.**: Amazon has consistently pushed the boundaries of corporate innovation, from its pioneering work in e-commerce to its dominance in cloud computing through Amazon Web Services (AWS). The company's culture of innovation is deeply embedded in its leadership principles, which emphasize customer obsession, long-term thinking, and continuous experimentation (Hitt et al., 2017, p. 157).

Innovation remains a fundamental driver of progress, but the context in which it occurs can significantly shape its trajectory. Corporate innovation, while sharing the same creative essence as general innovation, operates within a more complex, structured environment, requiring a strategic approach to align with organizational goals. The increasing emphasis on open innovation, digital transformation, and sustainability highlights the evolving nature of corporate innovation. Through careful navigation of internal and external challenges, companies can harness the power of innovation to maintain their competitive edge and drive long-term success.

1.2.2 Collaboration With Partners

Corporate collaborations and partnerships are integral to the different types and trends of corporate innovation outlined. Each approach heavily depends on strategic alliances with external entities to drive innovation and maintain a competitive edge. In essence, corporate collaboration and partnerships are the linchpins of these corporate innovation strategies. They enable companies to access vital new knowledge, technologies, and resources that are essential for driving innovation and maintaining relevance in a rapidly evolving market.

1.3 Open Innovation: The Cornerstone of Corporate Innovation

Open innovation (OI) traces its origins to the early 21st century, primarily through the work of Henry Chesbrough, who coined the term in his seminal book, *Open Innovation: The New Imperative for Creating and Profiting from Technology*, published in 2003. Chesbrough's work emerged from observing the limitations of traditional models of innovation, which were largely closed and relied heavily on internal research and development (R&D) within vertically integrated firms. This model, while successful for much of the 20th century, began to show cracks as global competition intensified and the pace of technological change accelerated.

Historically, large corporations like DuPont, IBM, and Xerox thrived by leveraging economies of scale and scope, as described by Alfred Chandler in his work on vertically integrated organizations. However, by the late 20th century, the innovation landscape began to shift. The rise of intermediate markets, venture capital, and startup ecosystems introduced new pathways for innovation, challenging the established theories of Chandler and others. Scholars like Arora, Gans, and Stern documented these changes, noting the emergence of alliances, networks, and intermediaries like InnoCentive, which connected problem solvers with solution seekers (Radziwon et al., 2023, p. 2).

Chesbrough's OI framework synthesized these disparate elements, advocating for a model where firms could and should use external ideas and paths to market alongside their internal efforts. This approach was revolutionary, as it encouraged companies to look beyond their boundaries for innovation, leveraging external knowledge and resources. The concept of OI gained traction as it provided a coherent framework to understand and harness these new dynamics, offering a Kuhnian paradigm shift in the way organisations approached innovation (Radziwon et al., 2023, p. 2).

1.3.1 Evolution and Current Trends

Since its introduction, OI has evolved significantly, adapting to the changing technological and economic landscape. In the early years, OI primarily focused on the technological sector, where rapid advancements and the proliferation of digital technologies created fertile ground for external collaborations. Companies began to recognize the value of tapping into external networks, including universities, research institutions, and even competitors, to drive innovation.

Over time, the principles of OI have permeated various industries beyond technology, including pharmaceuticals, consumer goods, and automotive sectors. This expansion reflects the versatility and adaptability of the OI framework, which can be tailored to different contexts and needs. For instance, Procter & Gamble's Connect + Develop program became a benchmark for OI, demonstrating how a consumer goods company could successfully integrate external innovations to drive growth (Radziwon et al., 2023, p. 3).

In recent years, the focus of OI has shifted toward integrating digital strategies and big data analytics, reflecting broader trends in the digital economy. The rise of platforms and ecosystems has further underscored the importance of open, collaborative approaches. Companies are increasingly leveraging digital platforms to crowdsource ideas, engage with external partners, and cocreate value. This trend highlights the ongoing evolution of OI as it adapts to the demands of a digital-first world.

Moreover, the COVID-19 pandemic accelerated the adoption of OI practices as organizations sought agile and resilient strategies to navigate unprecedented challenges. The need for rapid innovation and collaboration across borders and sectors underscored the relevance of OI in addressing complex, global issues.

Open innovation has transformed from a novel concept to a mainstream strategy that continues to evolve. Its ability to adapt to new contexts and integrate emerging technologies ensures its relevance in the ever-changing landscape of innovation. As organizations continue to face complex challenges, the principles of OI offer a robust framework for harnessing the collective intelligence and creativity of diverse networks (Radziwon et al., 2023, p. 4).

1.3.2 Open Innovation Challenges from Collaboration with Startups: A Human-Level Perspective

Collaboration with startups can invigorate established corporations like Samsung Electronics, with fresh ideas and innovative approaches. However, these collaborations also present unique challenges, particularly at the human level. Addressing these challenges is crucial to ensure successful partnerships and the seamless integration of external innovations into the corporation's strategic framework.

Cultural Differences: One of the most significant human-level challenges is the cultural difference between startups and large corporations. Startups often operate with a flat organizational structure, fostering a culture of agility, informality, and rapid decision-making. In contrast, large corporations like Samsung tend to have hierarchical structures, formal processes, and more bureaucratic decision-making pathways. These differences can lead to misunderstandings, misaligned expectations, and friction between the collaborating teams (Gassmann et al., 2010).

Trust and Relationship Building: Building trust is another critical challenge in collaborations with startups. Startups may be wary of sharing their innovative ideas and proprietary technologies, fearing appropriation or exploitation by the larger corporation. Conversely, corporate teams might be skeptical of the startup's reliability and capability to deliver on promises. Establishing mutual trust requires time, transparency, and consistent communication. Developing personal relationships and understanding the motivations and constraints of each partner can help bridge this trust gap (Chesbrough, 2011).

Communication Barriers: Effective communication is essential for any collaboration, yet it can be particularly challenging when partnering with startups. Differences in language, jargon, and communication styles can lead to misinterpretations and ineffective collaboration. Startups often communicate in a more informal and direct manner, while corporate environments may favor formal and structured communication. Bridging these communication gaps requires creating an environment where open and honest dialogue is encouraged and facilitated (Gassmann et al., 2010).

Alignment of Goals and Expectations: Aligning goals and expectations between startups and corporations can be challenging. Startups typically prioritize speed, innovation, and market disruption, while corporations might focus on stability, scalability, and integration with existing systems. Misalignment in objectives can lead to frustration and conflict. It is essential to have clear, upfront discussions about the goals, expectations, and success metrics for the collaboration. Regular check-ins and adaptive planning can help ensure that both parties remain aligned throughout the partnership (Lee & Yoo, 2010, p. 141).

Managing Differences in Work Pace and Processes: Startups operate at a rapid pace, often iterating quickly and adapting to market feedback with agility. Large corporations, on the other hand, might have more rigid processes and longer timelines for decision-making and implementation. This difference in work pace can cause frustration on both sides. Startups might perceive the corporation as slow and cumbersome, while the corporate team might view the startup as hasty and lacking in thoroughness. Finding a balance between these differing paces and processes requires flexibility and a willingness to adapt from both parties (Chesbrough, 2011).

Human Resource Management: Integrating startup teams into the corporate environment can pose human resource challenges. Differences in compensation structures, career progression, and workplace culture can affect employee morale and retention. Startups may have more flexible and creative work environments, while corporate settings might be more structured and formal. Ensuring that startup employees feel valued and integrated into the larger corporate culture is essential for maintaining motivation and productivity. Initiatives like joint training sessions, cross-functional teams, and cultural exchange programs can help in this integration process (Gassmann et al., 2010).

Power Dynamics: The inherent power imbalance between a large corporation and a smaller startup can also create challenges. Startups might feel overshadowed or dominated by the corporate partner, leading to a reluctance to voice concerns or propose innovative ideas. It is crucial for the corporation to create an inclusive and supportive environment where the startup feels empowered and valued as an equal partner. Encouraging open dialogue, respecting the startup's expertise, and involving them in strategic decision-making can mitigate these power dynamics (Lee & Yoo, 2010, p. 140).

While collaboration with startups offers significant innovation opportunities for corporations like Samsung Electronics, it also presents numerous human-level challenges. Addressing cultural differences, building trust, ensuring effective communication, aligning goals, managing work pace differences, handling human resource integration, and balancing power dynamics are all critical to building successful and productive partnerships. By focusing on these human-level factors, corporations can enhance their collaborative efforts and achieve mutually beneficial outcomes.

1.4 Coaching Strategies for Corporate Innovation

The challenges of sustainability, market relevance, and competition in the VUCA economy demand a fundamental shift in corporate strategies. Corporate innovation, when executed effectively, provides the tools to navigate these challenges and ensure long-term success. Companies prioritizing innovation increase their adaptability and establish themselves as leaders in a rapidly changing market. Current trends in corporate venturing, digital transformation, and sustainability and social innovation are all encompassed by the broader concept of open innovation.

Corporate innovation does not occur in isolation; it requires a deliberate strategy and a supportive organizational culture. Companies must nurture an environment that encourages experimentation, views failure as a learning opportunity, and rewards creative thinking. Leaders are crucial in setting the tone for innovation by championing new ideas and providing the necessary resources and support. Additionally, they must recognize the importance of collaboration within the organization and with external partners to drive innovation. However, partnerships with startups, in particular, can pose significant challenges, especially on a human level. Overcoming these challenges necessitates effective coaching as an intermediary, facilitating smoother collaborations and advancing innovation.

This book, *Coaching Strategies for Corporate Innovation: A Systemic Approach to Coaching Teams and Leaders*, provides the coaching strategies needed to bridge gaps in corporate innovation and cultivate a culture of collaboration and innovation.

Chapter 2

Coaching Innovation

Innovation in today's corporate landscape is not merely an option but a necessity. The rapid pace of technological advancement, market disruptions, and the ever-increasing need for sustainability have made it imperative for corporations to innovate continually. However, successful innovation requires more than just adopting new technologies or developing new products. It demands a profound cultural shift and a strategic approach to collaboration, notably when corporations engage with startups.

This chapter explores how coaching serves as a critical intermediary in corporate innovation, introducing three coaching innovation phases: matching innovation, collaborative innovation, and the ecosystem of innovation. Through these phases, we will examine in subsequent chapters coaching strategies to bridge the gap between corporate and startup cultures, cultivating an environment where innovation can thrive.

Key Takeaways

- **Corporate Innovation Requires a Cultural Shift:** Successful innovation extends beyond technology adoption to cultural transformation and strategic collaboration.
- **Open Innovation as a Competitive Advantage:** Samsung's success illustrates how external partnerships with universities, startups, and research institutions accelerate innovation and market leadership.
- **Navigating Corporate–Startup Challenges:** Coaches address issues like cultural integration, IP management, resource allocation, and strategic alignment to enhance collaboration.
- **Systemic Coaching Approach in Three Phases for Corporate–Startup Collaborations in Open Innovation:**
  - **Matching Innovation:** Aligning corporate and startup partners with a people-first approach.
  - **Collaborative Innovation:** Bridging cultural gaps, encouraging trust, and balancing agility with structure.

DOI: 10.4324/9781003469155-3

- **Ecosystem of Innovation:** Encouraging continuous adaptation, pivoting, and identifying new opportunities.
- **Coaching as an Innovation Enabler:** Coaching fosters trust, psychological safety, and alignment between personal and organizational goals, ensuring sustained engagement in innovation initiatives.
- **Developing Adaptive Leadership:** Coaches help leaders navigate change, manage resistance, and build a collaborative, innovation-driven culture.
- **Facilitating Collaborative Networks:** Coaching enhances knowledge-sharing and cross-functional collaboration, driving creativity and problem-solving.
- **Continuous Learning and Development:** Coaches instill a culture of continuous learning, enabling teams to adapt, refine strategies, and sustain innovation over time.
- **Sustainable Innovation Culture:** Coaches instill reflection, agility, and resilience, ensuring organizations remain competitive and forward-thinking.
- **Coaching as a Catalyst for Corporate Transformation:** Coaching drives strategic alignment, cultural synergy, and sustained innovation by integrating leadership development and strategic execution.

2.1 A Successful Corporate Innovation Through Open Collaboration

We begin by analyzing an example of an open innovation—Samsung—to have a sense of the nature of corporate innovation, in the form of open innovation.

Samsung Electronics' transformation through open innovation has played a pivotal role in its rise to the forefront of technological advancements. Recognizing the limitations of relying solely on internal R&D, Samsung adopted an open innovation strategy, collaborating extensively with external entities to drive its innovation agenda.

The company's decision to embrace open innovation emerged from the realization that external ideas and technologies could significantly enhance its innovation capabilities. Samsung initiated partnerships with universities, research institutions, and startups worldwide, fostering a collaborative ecosystem that spanned multiple continents. This global network allowed Samsung to tap into diverse pools of knowledge and expertise, accelerating its research and development processes (Lee & Yoo, 2010, p. 137).

To facilitate these collaborations, Samsung established innovation centers and accelerator programs designed to nurture and support external innovations. These centers served as hubs where academia, industry experts, and startups could converge to work on cutting-edge projects. By providing resources, mentorship, and funding, Samsung empowered these external partners to bring their ideas to fruition. This symbiotic relationship not only benefited the collaborators but also enriched Samsung's product pipeline with innovative solutions (Lee & Yoo, 2010, p. 139).

One notable example of Samsung's successful open innovation practice is its collaboration with global universities. By funding research projects and engaging in joint ventures, Samsung gained access to groundbreaking research in areas such as semiconductors, artificial intelligence, and telecommunications. This proactive approach allowed Samsung to stay ahead of technological trends and incorporate state-of-the-art innovations into its product offerings. For instance, Samsung's collaboration with Stanford University led to advancements in nanotechnology that were pivotal in enhancing semiconductor performance (Chesbrough, 2011).

In addition to academic partnerships, Samsung actively engaged with startups through its accelerator programs, which provided startups with the necessary infrastructure and support to develop their technologies. This initiative not only helped startups scale their innovations but also allowed Samsung to identify and integrate promising technologies early in their development stages. This strategy proved particularly effective in areas like mobile technology and consumer electronics, where rapid innovation cycles are crucial (Lee & Yoo, 2010, p. 141). As another example, the Samsung NEXT program invests in startups and integrates their cutting-edge technologies into Samsung's product lines (Samsung NEXT, 2020).

Moreover, Samsung's open innovation strategy extended to strategic acquisitions and investments. By acquiring companies with complementary technologies and investing in promising startups, Samsung bolstered its innovation portfolio. These strategic moves enabled Samsung to diversify its technological capabilities and strengthen its position in competitive markets. For example, the acquisition of Harman International expanded Samsung's capabilities in connected car technologies and audio systems, areas that are critical for the future of consumer electronics (Samsung Electronics, 2017).

Samsung's commitment to open innovation has had a profound impact on its growth and success. The company's ability to harness external innovations has resulted in groundbreaking products and technologies, solidifying its leadership in the tech industry. By fostering a culture of collaboration and openness, Samsung has created a dynamic innovation ecosystem that continually propels it forward.

Samsung Electronics' transformation through open innovation demonstrates the power of external collaborations in driving technological advancement. By partnering with universities, research institutions, and startups, Samsung has effectively expanded its innovation capacity, ensuring its continued dominance in semiconductors, consumer electronics, and telecommunications. This strategic shift from a closed to an open innovation model serves as a valuable lesson for other companies aiming to enhance their innovation capabilities and stay competitive in today's fast-paced technological landscape.

2.1.1 Insights

From the case study on Samsung's successful open innovation initiative, many insights can be highlighted from the coaching perspective.

The transformation of Samsung Electronics through open innovation underscores the potential for significant technological advancements when external collaborations are effectively harnessed. The case study reveals numerous inherent complexities in managing such collaborations, which, if not adequately addressed, could hinder the desired outcomes. The success of Samsung's open innovation initiatives hinges on navigating challenges like cultural integration, intellectual property management, and strategic alignment. By identifying these issues, targeted coaching can play a pivotal role in enhancing the effectiveness of these initiatives. The following are the issues identified:

1 **Cultural Integration**: Ensuring seamless integration between Samsung's internal culture and the diverse cultures of external partners, such as universities, startups, and research institutions.
2 **Collaborative Synergy**: Facilitating effective collaboration between Samsung's internal teams and external entities to ensure alignment in goals, expectations, and project timelines.
3 **Resource Allocation**: Guiding Samsung in balancing resources (funding, mentorship, infrastructure) between internal R&D and external innovation efforts to maximize the impact of both.
4 **Intellectual Property (IP) Management**: Navigating the complexities of IP sharing and protection when working with multiple external partners to avoid conflicts and ensure mutual benefits.
5 **Innovation Ecosystem Management**: Coaching Samsung on how to manage and sustain a dynamic and global innovation ecosystem that includes academia, startups, and industry experts.
6 **Change Management**: Assisting Samsung in managing internal resistance to open innovation practices, especially among teams accustomed to a traditional, closed innovation approach.
7 **Leadership in Open Innovation**: Developing leadership skills focused on fostering an environment of openness, trust, and collaboration with external partners.
8 **Risk Management**: Addressing the risks associated with open innovation, including dependency on external innovations and the potential dilution of Samsung's core competencies.
9 **Strategic Alignment**: Ensuring that the open innovation initiatives are strategically aligned with Samsung's long-term business goals and market position.
10 **Talent Management and Development**: Coaching Samsung on attracting, retaining, and developing talent that can work within an open innovation framework, including managing diverse teams across geographies.

11 **Evaluation and Integration of External Innovations**: Providing guidance on the processes and criteria for evaluating external innovations and integrating them effectively into Samsung's existing product lines.

12 **Communication and Stakeholder Management**: Enhancing communication strategies to effectively manage relationships with various stakeholders involved in the open innovation ecosystem.

13 **Scalability of Innovations**: Coaching on how to scale successful external innovations across Samsung's global operations, ensuring consistency in quality and market readiness.

The list of issues is derived from a combination of theoretical frameworks and practical insights found in the literature on open innovation, innovation management, and corporate transformation. The basis for the list includes established principles of open innovation, challenges commonly associated with collaborative innovation efforts, and best practices in managing external partnerships.

2.1.2 Basis for the List of Issues

1 **Open Innovation Frameworks**: The concept of open innovation, introduced by Henry Chesbrough, emphasizes the challenges and opportunities of integrating external knowledge into a company's innovation processes. Issues such as cultural integration, intellectual property (IP) management, and risk management are central to this framework. Chesbrough (2011) discusses these elements, highlighting how they are essential for a successful open innovation strategy (p. 47).

2 **Innovation Ecosystem Management**: Managing a global innovation ecosystem requires careful attention to collaboration, resource allocation, and strategic alignment. These are well-documented challenges in the literature on innovation ecosystems. Adner (2006) explains that companies must align their innovation strategies with the broader ecosystem to ensure success, making ecosystem management a critical area for coaching (p. 105).

3 **Leadership and Change Management in Innovation**: Effective leadership in an open innovation environment is crucial. Leaders must foster collaboration, manage organizational change, and ensure that external innovations align with the company's long-term strategic goals. West and Bogers (2014) discuss the importance of leadership in managing the complexities of open innovation and driving change within organizations (p. 818).

4 **Strategic and Operational Challenges**: Implementing open innovation involves numerous practical challenges, such as evaluating external innovations, integrating them into existing product lines, and scaling them across global operations. Gassmann, Enkel, and Chesbrough (2010)

explore these operational aspects, emphasizing the need for companies to address these issues through structured processes and clear criteria for innovation integration (p. 215).

The Samsung Electronics' transformation illustrates the potential and, at the same time, the challenges in executing open innovation successfully. Samsung's open innovation initiative clearly showed how external collaborations can catalyze technological breakthroughs and strategic growth while exposing challenges. Challenges, or issues, such as cultural integration, intellectual property management, strategic misalignment, and ecosystem coordination. These issues can be elevated or minimized with coaching, where coaches can play a role in addressing these challenges by equipping organizations with the leadership acumen, strategic clarity, and change management competencies necessary to excel in an open innovation framework. Through targeted guidance, organizations can navigate the complexities of open innovation with greater confidence and effectiveness, reinforcing their capacity to achieve long-term success.

2.2 Overcoming Challenges in Corporate Innovation Through Coaching

An innovation coach can play a pivotal role in addressing the various challenges in corporate-startup collaborations by leveraging the principles outlined in Hollywood et al.'s (2016) holistic coaching framework. Here's how:

1   **Cultivating Cultural Awareness and Sensitivity:** The innovation coach can act as an intermediary who cultivates cultural awareness and sensitivity between the corporate and startup teams. By facilitating open dialogues, the coach can help both parties articulate their expectations, values, and working styles. Hollywood et al. (2016) emphasize the importance of creating an environment where individuals feel safe to express their thoughts and concerns. The coach can organize workshops or team-building activities that promote understanding and respect for each other's cultural backgrounds, thereby reducing the likelihood of misunderstandings and fostering collaboration (Hollywood et al., 2016, p. 35).

2   **Developing Adaptive Leadership:** The innovation coach can guide leaders from both the corporate and startup sides to adopt adaptive leadership practices. Hollywood et al. (2016) highlight the role of coaching in developing leaders who can navigate complexity and uncertainty. The coach can provide personalized coaching sessions that focus on enhancing leaders' ability to flex their leadership styles according to the situation. This might include helping corporate leaders become more open to risk-taking and less hierarchical, while encouraging startup leaders to appreciate the need for structure and process in certain situations (Hollywood et al., 2016, p. 41).

3 **Facilitating the Creation of a Shared Vision and Goals:** The innovation coach can facilitate the development of a shared vision and clear goals between the corporate and startup teams. By aligning personal aspirations with organizational objectives, as suggested by Hollywood et al. (2016), the coach can ensure that both parties are working towards a common purpose. The coach might use collaborative workshops to cocreate a vision that resonates with both cultures, ensuring that it is both strategic and personally meaningful. This shared vision can then serve as a touchstone for decision-making and conflict resolution, helping to transcend cultural differences (Hollywood et al., 2016, p. 38).

4 **Supporting Continuous Learning and Development**: Finally, the innovation coach can encourage a culture of continuous learning and development, which is crucial for managing cultural clashes and fostering innovation. Hollywood et al. (2016) emphasize the importance of ongoing development in sustaining innovation. The coach can introduce practices like reflective learning sessions, where both corporate and startup teams can share experiences, learn from each other, and apply new insights to their work. This continuous learning process can help both sides adapt to each other's cultures over time, reducing friction and enhancing collaboration (Hollywood et al., 2016, p. 44).

By applying a holistic coaching approach, the innovation coach can bridge the cultural gap between corporates and startups. The coach's role in fostering cultural awareness, developing adaptive leadership, aligning visions, and promoting continuous learning ensures that both parties can collaborate effectively, leveraging cultural strengths to drive innovation.

2.3 Coaching Innovation for Corporate Innovation (Open Innovation)

2.3.1 Coaching Innovation: The Philosophy

The philosophy of coaching innovation is rooted in essential principles that shape the interactions between coaches and their clients, particularly within the context of corporate–startup collaborations. This philosophy strongly emphasizes cultivating a culture of innovation, adaptability, and trust—elements that are indispensable for achieving successful outcomes in these partnerships.

At the core of coaching innovation is the belief that collaboration and cocreation are fundamental to the innovation process. This approach aligns with Chesbrough's (2003) research on open innovation, which underscores the critical importance of cocreation between corporate teams and startups. Coaches play a pivotal role in facilitating this collaborative environment, helping to dismantle organizational silos and encouraging the exchange of diverse perspectives. This collaborative ethos is about working together and creating a synergy that often leads to groundbreaking innovations (Chesbrough, 2003, p. 36).

In addition to fostering collaboration, coaching innovation's philosophy strongly emphasizes empowerment and autonomy. Dweck's (2006) concept of the growth mindset is particularly relevant here, as it highlights the importance of fostering a sense of autonomy and self-efficacy within innovation teams. Coaches are instrumental in cultivating this environment, enabling team members to take the initiative and contribute their unique insights confidently. This empowerment is not merely about individual confidence but about creating a culture where each member feels capable of driving innovation forward (Dweck, 2006, p. 25).

The adaptability and continuous learning principles are central to the coaching innovation philosophy. Adapting to changing market dynamics and technological advancements is crucial in today's rapidly evolving business landscape. Senge's (1990) concept of the learning organization provides a theoretical foundation for this principle, emphasizing the need for continuous learning and adaptability. Coaches encourage teams to embrace a growth mindset, where learning from both successes and failures becomes a driving force behind innovation. This adaptability is not just a response to change but a proactive approach to navigating the complexities of innovation (Senge, 1990, p. 57).

Furthermore, establishing trust and psychological safety is a cornerstone of effective coaching in innovation contexts. Edmondson's (1999) research on psychological safety provides valuable insights into how trust enables team members to take risks, express their ideas openly, and challenge the status quo without fear of negative repercussions. Coaches play a crucial role in creating an environment that encourages psychological safety, which in turn enhances creativity and leads to more effective collaboration. This focus on trust is not just about mitigating fear but about creating a foundation where innovative ideas can flourish (Edmondson, 1999, p. 354).

The philosophy of coaching innovation encompasses the holistic development of individuals and teams. Goleman's (1995) work on emotional intelligence underscores the importance of developing interpersonal skills alongside technical expertise. Coaches focus on building competencies such as communication, empathy, and conflict resolution, ensuring that teams are well equipped to handle the complexities of collaborative innovation (Goleman, 1995, p. 96).

To further enhance these philosophical underpinnings, coaches employ formulation techniques. Formulation, as described by Lane et al. (2025), provides a structured method for understanding a client's presenting issues by considering their situational context, recurring patterns, and overall case dynamics. By applying formulation, coaches gain a more nuanced appreciation of the client's challenges and can tailor their approach to better align with the client's specific needs and goals. This integration allows coaches to create a safe environment where their clients' innovative ideas can flourish (Lane et al., 2025, p. 12).

The philosophy of coaching innovation is integral to effective corporate–startup collaborations. By emphasizing the interconnected principles of collaboration, empowerment, adaptability, trust, and holistic development, coaches can significantly enhance the innovation process, ultimately leading to successful outcomes in open innovation initiatives.

2.3.2 Coaching Approach

Coaching can serve as a powerful innovation intermediary by facilitating and sustaining organizational change, as outlined in the article "Holistic Mentoring and Coaching to Sustain Organisational Change and Innovation" by Hollywood et al. (2016). The authors discuss how a holistic approach to mentoring and coaching can support both the personal and professional development of individuals, thereby fostering an environment conducive to continuous innovation.

1 **Building Trust and Psychological Safety:** Coaching helps establish a foundation of trust and psychological safety, which are critical for innovation. Hollywood et al. (2016) argue that when individuals feel safe to express their ideas without fear of judgment or retribution, they are more likely to engage in creative thinking and take the risks necessary for innovation. Coaches act as intermediaries by creating this environment, encouraging open communication and the free exchange of ideas (Hollywood et al., 2016, p. 35).
2 **Aligning Personal and Organizational Goals:** The holistic coaching approach advocated by Hollywood et al. (2016) emphasizes the alignment of personal aspirations with organizational objectives. Coaches help individuals understand how their contributions align with the broader goals of the organization, which can drive motivation and commitment to innovation efforts. By bridging the gap between personal and organizational goals, coaches ensure that innovation initiatives are not only strategically aligned but also personally meaningful for the individuals involved (Hollywood et al., 2016, p. 38).
3 **Developing Adaptive Leadership Skills:** Innovation often requires leaders to adapt quickly to changing circumstances and to lead teams through uncertainty. Hollywood et al. (2016) highlight the role of coaching in developing these adaptive leadership skills. Through targeted coaching sessions, leaders learn to navigate the complexities of organizational change, manage resistance, and inspire their teams to embrace innovation. This development of leadership capacity is crucial for sustaining long-term innovation (Hollywood et al., 2016, p. 41).
4 **Facilitating Collaborative Networks:** The article points out that innovation thrives in collaborative environments where knowledge and ideas can flow freely across boundaries. Coaches can act as intermediaries by facilitating these networks, helping to connect individuals and teams who may not typically interact. This cross-pollination of ideas is essential for

generating novel solutions and sustaining innovation within the organization (Hollywood et al., 2016, p. 43).

5 **Supporting Continuous Learning and Development:**Hollywood et al. (2016) argue that continuous learning is vital for sustaining innovation. Coaches play a key role in fostering a culture of learning by encouraging individuals to seek out new knowledge, reflect on their experiences, and apply their learning to new challenges. This ongoing development not only enhances individual capabilities but also contributes to the overall innovation capacity of the organization (Hollywood et al., 2016, p. 44).

Formulation complements this holistic approach by offering a systematic understanding of the factors influencing an individual's or team's innovation journey. Coaches use formulation to identify underlying beliefs, patterns of behavior, and contextual factors that may hinder or support the innovation process (Corrie & Kovacs, 2019, p. 142). Using formulation, coaches effectively engage with the client, tailoring their interventions to address specific challenges and leverage unique strengths.

By adopting this comprehensive approach, coaching becomes more than just a tool for individual development; it becomes a strategic intermediary that aligns personal and organizational goals, develops adaptive leadership, facilitates collaboration, and promotes continuous learning. These elements are essential for creating and sustaining an innovative culture within organizations.

2.4 Coaching Innovation: The Three Phases Acting as Intermediaries in Corporate Innovation

Coaching plays a pivotal role in corporate innovation, acting as a catalyst that facilitates the alignment of diverse cultures, values, and goals. In the context of corporate–startup collaborations, coaching strategies must address the inherent challenges that arise from the clash of corporate and startup cultures. Corporations, with their established processes and risk-averse nature, often find themselves at odds with startups that operate with agility, flexibility, and a high tolerance for risk. This cultural clash can hinder collaboration and stifle innovation. Therefore, coaches must adopt a systemic approach that synthesizes various elements of innovation into a cohesive framework.

For coaching innovation, three related and distinctive phases—matching innovation, collaborative innovation, and ecosystem innovation—will illustrate the coaching strategies for corporate innovation.

2.4.1 Matching Innovation

Matching innovation is the first phase of the systemic approach to coaching corporate–startup collaborations. It emphasizes the importance of aligning the right people and organizations before focusing on technology.

1 **People Before Technology:** The success of any innovation initiative depends on the people involved. Therefore, selecting the right startup founders and matching them with the appropriate corporate entity is crucial. The concept of "people before technology" underscores the importance of evaluating the compatibility of the startup founder's vision, values, and leadership style with those of the corporation. Coaching strategies in this context should focus on assessing the character traits of the startup founder, such as authenticity, humility, and resilience. These traits play a critical role in determining the founder's ability to navigate the complexities of corporate collaborations. For example, a startup founder who exhibits humility may be more open to feedback and collaboration, while resilience ensures perseverance in the face of setbacks (Brown, 2018, p. 45). Coaches must guide corporate leaders in identifying these traits during the selection process, ensuring a good match between the startup and the corporate entity.

2 **Shared Vision, Shared Dreams:** Once the right people are in place, the next step is to align the team's vision, values, and goals. A shared vision acts as a unifying force that drives the collaboration forward. However, aligning the visions of two distinct entities—each with its own goals and aspirations—can be challenging. Coaching strategies should facilitate open and honest communication between the corporate leaders and startup founders to establish a shared vision. Coaches can employ techniques such as visioning workshops and collaborative goal-setting sessions to create a common ground. These strategies not only help in aligning the team's vision but also in fostering a sense of ownership and commitment among all members (Goleman, 2000, p. 32). The result is a cohesive team that is driven by a shared purpose, which is essential for the success of any innovation initiative.

2.4.2 Collaborative Innovation

Collaborative innovation is the second phase of the systemic approach, focusing on the integration of corporate and startup cultures. The success of any collaboration depends on the ability of both parties to work together effectively, despite their differences.

1 **Culture Is Key:** Cultural integration is perhaps the most significant challenge in corporate–startup collaborations. Corporations often operate within a structured and hierarchical framework, while startups thrive in a more flexible and dynamic environment. These differences can lead to misunderstandings, miscommunications, and, ultimately, a breakdown in collaboration.

2 Coaching strategies should focus on bridging these cultural gaps by fostering mutual understanding and respect. Coaches can facilitate cross-cultural

training sessions that help both parties understand each other's work styles, decision-making processes, and communication preferences (Schein, 2010, p. 56). Additionally, coaches should encourage the adoption of a hybrid culture that combines the best of both worlds—corporate discipline with startup agility. This hybrid approach can create an environment where innovation can flourish, as it allows for flexibility and speed while maintaining a level of structure and accountability.

3   **Trust Before Collaboration:** Trust forms the foundation of any successful collaboration. Without trust, even the most well-matched teams will struggle to innovate together. Building trust, however, requires time and effort, especially in a corporate-startup collaboration where the stakes are high, and the risks are significant.

4   Coaching strategies should prioritize trust-building activities that encourage transparency, open communication, and mutual respect. Coaches can facilitate trust-building exercises, such as team-building workshops and collaborative problem-solving sessions, which help in creating a safe space for innovation (Covey, 2006, p. 74). By establishing trust early in the collaboration, teams are more likely to work together effectively, share ideas openly, and take calculated risks— all of which are essential for driving innovation.

2.4.3 Ecosystem of Innovation

The third phase of the systemic approach is the ecosystem of innovation, which addresses the broader context in which corporate–startup collaborations take place. This includes the external environment, industry trends, and the future possibilities that emerge from the collaboration.

1   **Progressive Pivoting:** In the fast-paced world of innovation, the ability to pivot quickly in response to changing technologies and market conditions is crucial. Progressive pivoting refers to the continuous learning and adaptation that is necessary for staying ahead of the curve.

2   Coaching strategies should focus on fostering a culture of continuous learning and adaptability within the innovation team. Coaches can encourage the adoption of agile methodologies that allow for iterative development and quick adjustments based on feedback (Rigby et al., 2016, p. 20). Additionally, coaches should guide teams in anticipating industry disruptions and exploring new opportunities for innovation. By embracing a mindset of progressive pivoting, teams can remain flexible and responsive, ensuring their continued relevance in a rapidly changing environment

3   **An Emergent Role:** As corporate–startup collaborations evolve, new roles and opportunities may emerge. The ability to identify and capitalize on these opportunities is key to the long-term success of the collaboration.

4   Coaching strategies should help teams navigate the uncertainties and ambiguities that come with innovation. Coaches can facilitate scenario planning sessions that explore potential future outcomes and identify emerging trends (Schwartz, 1991, p. 38). By helping teams think beyond the immediate goals of the collaboration, coaches can inspire them to envision new possibilities and roles that may arise in the future. This forward-thinking approach ensures that the collaboration remains dynamic and adaptable, with the potential to create lasting impact.

Coaching innovation is not a one-size-fits-all approach; it requires a nuanced understanding of the complexities involved in corporate-startup collaborations. By adopting a systemic approach that synthesizes matching innovation, collaborative innovation, and the ecosystem of innovation, coaches can effectively bridge the cultural and organizational gaps that often hinder innovation. The strategies outlined in this chapter provide a road map for coaches to navigate these challenges and foster an environment where innovation can thrive. In doing so, they play a crucial role in driving corporate innovation and ensuring the success of corporate–startup collaborations.

Part II

The Matching Innovation

Chapter 3

Founder Before Technology

In corporate open innovation, selecting startups for collaboration or investment requires a multifaceted approach. While technological innovation remains crucial, corporations must consider comprehensive criteria to ensure successful partnerships. These criteria encompass the startup's technological offerings, business model, market potential, and alignment with corporate objectives.

From a corporate open innovation perspective, critical criteria for startup selection include the relevance to the company's needs, innovation and disruptive potential, quality of the business model, and technical feasibility. The experience and skills of the founding team play a vital role, as does the cultural fit between the startup and the corporation. Market potential and alignment with strategic objectives are equally important, ensuring collaboration contributes to long-term corporate goals. Risk assessment and impact measurement mechanisms round out the evaluation process, providing a holistic view of the potential partnership (StartUs Insights, n.d.; Weiblen & Chesbrough, 2015). This comprehensive approach to startup selection reflects the complex nature of open innovation in today's business landscape.

Why "people before technology"? In this chapter, *people* are the startup founders, and *technology* means technology and technology-related criteria. These include relevance to the company's needs, innovation and disruptive potential, business model quality, technical feasibility, market potential, alignment with strategic objectives, and impact measurement (StartUs Insights, n.d.). These factors are often technology driven or heavily influenced by technological advancements, reflecting the increasing importance of digital and technological innovations in modern business strategies.

The allure of cutting-edge technology often overshadows a crucial factor: the people behind the startups. While technological prowess undoubtedly plays a pivotal role, corporate leaders must prioritize the human element when selecting startups for their innovation programs. The startup founders' character-based leadership traits, emotional intelligence, and coachability form the bedrock of successful collaboration, often surpassing the importance of the technology itself.

Corporate open innovation programs have traditionally focused on criteria such as market potential, technical feasibility, and strategic alignment

DOI: 10.4324/9781003469155-5

(Weiblen & Chesbrough, 2015). However, this technology-centric approach overlooks the indispensable role of the startup's leadership in driving innovation and ensuring long-term success. A groundbreaking technology in the hands of an inflexible, emotionally unintelligent founder may falter, while a less advanced solution guided by an adaptable, emotionally astute leader could flourish.

The emphasis on people aligns with the growing recognition of emotional intelligence as a critical factor in business success. Goleman (1998) argues that emotional intelligence accounts for 67% of the abilities deemed necessary for superior performance in leaders and matters twice as much as technical expertise or IQ. In the context of startup–corporate collaborations, this underscores the need to evaluate founders' interpersonal skills, self-awareness, and ability to navigate complex corporate environments.

Moreover, startup founders' coachability significantly influences the success of open innovation initiatives. Ries (2011) emphasizes the importance of a "learn and pivot" mindset in entrepreneurship. Founders who demonstrate openness to feedback, willingness to adapt, and capacity to learn from corporate partners are more likely to navigate collaboration challenges successfully.

Corporate leaders can enhance resilient and adaptive partnerships by prioritizing people over technology. This approach does not negate technological innovation's importance but complements it. A symbiosis of visionary leadership and technological acumen creates a fertile ground for transformative innovation.

As corporations embark on open innovation journeys, they must recalibrate their selection criteria to place greater weight on human factors. This paradigm shift promises to yield more fruitful collaborations, driving innovation that transcends technological boundaries and creates lasting value for both startups and corporations alike. The success of open innovation initiatives hinges on the delicate balance between human ingenuity and technological advancement, with the scales tipping slightly in favor of the former. The lens will focus on the startup founders in this chapter.

Key Takeaways

- **Founder Compatibility Matters:** Aligning a founder's leadership style and vision with corporate objectives is critical for long-term successful collaboration in corporate innovation.
- **Character Over Technology:** Traits like integrity, resilience, and adaptability outweigh technological advantages in ensuring sustainable collaborations.
- **Risks of Misalignment:** Poor founder selection can result in leadership failures, ethical issues, and failed collaborations.
- **Coaching as a Bridge:** Effective coaching helps align expectations, mediate conflicts, and enhance corporate–startup integration.
- **Critical Leadership Traits:** Founders with authenticity, humility, and adaptability create stronger, more resilient startups.

- **Lessons From Failures:** The collapses of Ofo and Quibi illustrate how leadership shortcomings can override technological promise.
- **Emotional Intelligence Drives Success:** Founders with high emotional intelligence foster collaboration and navigate corporate environments effectively.
- **Coachability as a Success Factor:** Founders who accept feedback and adapt have higher chances of succeeding in corporate partnerships.
- **Beyond Technology Evaluation:** Corporates must assess founders' leadership potential, ethical standards, and strategic vision.
- **Building Ethical Foundations:** Strong character-based leadership promotes transparency, accountability, and trust.
- **Resilience in Leadership:** Founders who persist through challenges sustain partnerships and drive long-term innovation.
- **Nubank's Success Story:** David Vélez's leadership at Nubank demonstrates how character-driven leadership fuels sustainable growth.
- **Theranos as a Cautionary Tale:** The founders' leadership failure accentuates the necessity of integrity in corporate-startup collaborations.
- **Strategic Coaching for Vision Alignment:** Coaching sessions help founders and corporate teams establish clear goals and shared objectives.
- **Self-Awareness Through Coaching:** Reflective coaching enhances founders' understanding of their leadership impact, improving corporate integration.

3.1 The Challenges: The Undermined Founder

Many high-profile failures in open innovation share a common thread: the overlooked weaknesses of the startup founders. Issues such as inadequate leadership skills, ethical lapses, and an inability to scale the business can undermine even the most promising technologies. Understanding these pitfalls is crucial for fostering successful corporate–startup collaborations (Christensen et al., 2015).

Ofo, a Chinese bike-sharing startup, offers critical lessons on the importance of effective leadership and sustainable growth management. Initially praised for its innovative urban mobility solution, Ofo rapidly expanded but soon encountered severe challenges. The company's aggressive growth strategy led to strained relationships with investors and partners, logistical issues, and financial instability (Bao & Lin, 2019b; Sun & Zhang, 2020).

Founder Dai Wei's leadership played a significant role in Ofo's trajectory. His vision fueled the company's initial success, but his inability to manage complexities and financial challenges proved detrimental. Dai's approach to financial management, characterized by overexpansion and lack of transparency, undermined stakeholder trust and stability (Chen & Chang, 2018; Zhou & Wu, 2019). Moreover, his leadership style lacked authenticity and humility, essential for navigating crises and maintaining effective partnerships.

Ofo's collapse highlights the necessity of robust and character-based leadership for long-term success. While innovation and vision are crucial, managing relationships, ensuring financial stability, and demonstrating authentic leadership are equally important (Bao & Lin, 2019b; Chen & Chang, 2018).

Quibi, a short-form streaming service founded by Jeffrey Katzenberg and led by CEO Meg Whitman, was launched in April 2020, with nearly $1.75 billion in funding and backing from industry giants. Despite this substantial support, Quibi shut down in October 2020, only six months later (Lev-Ram, 2020; Sherman, 2020). The platform faced significant collaboration challenges, particularly its rigid 10-minute episode format and lack of user engagement data, which led to a disconnect between Quibi's offerings and audience preferences (Vlessing, 2020). Additionally, the COVID-19 pandemic shifted consumer behavior toward long-form content, while Quibi's short-form model struggled to gain traction against established streaming services and platforms like TikTok (Spangler, 2020).

The leadership at Quibi exhibited a lack of adaptability and humility, crucial traits in character-based leadership. Katzenberg and Whitman persisted with their original vision despite mounting evidence of its flaws, demonstrating inflexibility and a disconnect from user needs. Effective leadership requires resilience and a willingness to pivot in response to market feedback—qualities notably absent at Quibi. Quibi's downfall underscores the importance of adaptable, empathetic leadership in guiding innovative ventures.

3.2 The Cost of Misalignment: Why Founder Selection Matters

Startups fail for numerous reasons, but patterns emerge when examining these failures closely. Poor leadership, lack of market understanding, inability to pivot, and ethical issues are common culprits. Founders play a pivotal role in these areas, significantly influencing the startup's trajectory (Gans et al., 2019).

We have seen from the examples of Ofo and Quibi the immense challenges startups face in operating their businesses. The relentless demands on the leaderships of the startup founders. And, inadvertently, the failures. Choosing the wrong founder can have far-reaching consequences. Misaligned values, poor leadership, and a lack of vision can stymie collaboration efforts. Corporates must recognize that the founder's character and leadership style will significantly impact the partnership's success (Roberts & Eesley, 2009).

To further emphasize the critical importance of selecting the right startup founders, this section presents an in-depth analysis of a relevant case study.

3.2.1 The Downfall of a Promising Health-Tech Startup

Background: In the early 2000s, a promising health-tech startup emerged, aiming to revolutionize the medical diagnostics industry. With a compelling vision, the company attracted massive investments and widespread media attention. The founder, a charismatic and ambitious entrepreneur, quickly became a Silicon Valley icon, often compared to Steve Jobs for the founder's vision and determination (Carreyrou, 2018).

The Vision: The startup promised to simplify blood testing, making it less invasive and more accessible. The founder envisioned a device that could run comprehensive tests with just a few drops of blood, thus transforming the healthcare landscape. This innovation promised to eliminate the need for large blood samples and extensive labwork, potentially saving lives through early detection of diseases (Macmillan Publishers, n.d.).

Rapid Rise: Investors poured millions into the startup, driven by the founder's persuasive pitch and her relentless drive. Major corporations and influential individuals joined the board, further bolstering the company's credibility. The startup's valuation soared, reaching billions of dollars within a few years. The founder became a media darling, gracing the covers of prestigious magazines and speaking at high-profile conferences (Carreyrou, 2018).

The Cracks Appear: Despite the outward success, internal reports began to indicate that the technology did not work as promised. Employees raised concerns about the accuracy and reliability of the blood tests. However, the founder dismissed these concerns and pressured employees to stay silent or face termination. The company continued to claim breakthroughs despite struggling to produce reliable results (Carreyrou, 2018).

Unravelling the Deception: Journalists and former employees started to uncover discrepancies in the company's claims. Investigative reports revealed that the startup had used commercial machines to run tests instead of its proprietary technology. Moreover, the founder and executives had misled investors, regulators, and patients about the efficacy and readiness of their product (Macmillan Publishers, n.d.).

Consequences: Regulatory bodies launched investigations, eventually exposing the full extent of the deception. Lawsuits followed, and the company's valuation plummeted. Investors lost millions, and patients who had relied on the flawed technology felt betrayed. The startup eventually shut down, marking one of the most dramatic failures in Silicon Valley history (Carreyrou, 2018).

Unpacking the Reasons Behind Failure

1   **Character Analysis:** The founder's character flaws were pivotal in the startup's downfall. Her inability to accept criticism and her relentless pursuit of success at any cost reflected a lack of integrity. She displayed a concerning level of hubris, believing her vision justified bending the truth. This behavior highlights a significant shortcoming in authenticity, as she presented a façade of infallibility while concealing fundamental technological flaws (Carreyrou, 2018).

Integrity involves honesty and strong moral principles, while authenticity requires being true to oneself and others. The founder's actions showcased a profound disregard for both. By misleading investors, regulators, and the public, she demonstrated a willingness to sacrifice ethical standards for personal and professional gain (Macmillan Publishers, n.d.).

2   **Culture of Deceit:** The founder's character shortcomings created a toxic culture within the company. Her insistence on maintaining the illusion of success at all costs led to a pervasive culture of deceit. Employees felt pressured to conform to unrealistic expectations, fearing retribution if they voiced concerns. This environment stifled innovation and fostered dishonesty, ultimately leading to the company's collapse (Carreyrou, 2018).

The company's failure underscores the importance of integrity and authenticity in leadership. Leaders must prioritize ethical standards and foster a culture of openness and accountability. Without these qualities, even the most promising ventures can fall victim to the corrosive effects of deceit.

3   **Revelation:** Theranos was the startup in question, The founder's story is a cautionary tale about the dangers of prioritizing image over substance and the critical importance of maintaining integrity and authenticity in pursuing innovation.

Theranos shows what happens when a charismatic founder with questionable ethics leads a startup. Its founder captivated investors and corporate partners with vision of revolutionizing blood testing. However, the founder's lack of transparency and ethical breaches led to one of the biggest corporate scandals in recent history. The technology, though promising, was overshadowed by the founder's flaws (Christensen et al., 2015).

3.2.2 Nubank—An Example of a Startup Founder of Strong Character

David Vélez's journey to founding Nubank is a compelling narrative of transforming personal frustration into a banking revolution. Born in Medellín, Colombia, and raised in Costa Rica, Vélez's diverse background influenced his innovative mindset (Forbes, 2020). His academic journey led him to Stanford University, where he earned degrees in engineering and an MBA, blending technical knowledge with business acumen (Stanford Graduate School of Business, 2021).

Vélez's professional career began in investment banking at Morgan Stanley, followed by roles at General Atlantic and Sequoia Capital (TechCrunch, 2019). These experiences sharpened his skills in the financial sector. In 2012, Vélez relocated to Brazil and encountered the inefficiencies of the local banking system, sparking the idea for Nubank (Forbes, 2020). In 2013, with Cristina Junqueira and Edward Wible, he cofounded Nubank in São Paulo, introducing a no-fee credit card managed via a mobile app. This innovation resonated with Brazil's tech-savvy youth, eager for change in their banking experiences (Reuters, 2018).

Despite facing a challenging regulatory environment and consumer skepticism, Vélez's relentless focus on customer experience and cutting-edge technology paid off (Reuters, 2018). Under his leadership, Nubank's user-friendly app gained a loyal customer base. Vélez's visionary thinking, resilience, humility, and integrity drove Nubank's success (TechCrunch, 2019). He navigated regulatory hurdles, prioritized seamless and transparent banking, and fostered a diverse, inclusive company culture (Stanford Graduate School of Business, 2021). His humility allowed him to personally connect with employees and customers, while his integrity ensured stakeholder trust and loyalty.

Vélez's coachability and emotional intelligence have been critical to his success. His openness to feedback and willingness to learn enabled him to adapt quickly to new challenges. Vélez's emotional intelligence helped him understand and manage his emotions while navigating interpersonal relationships. This trait was essential in building a solid team and creating a positive work environment (Forbes, 2020).

In 2018, a landmark moment occurred when Tencent invested $180 million in Nubank, providing essential capital and access to technological expertise (Reuters, 2018). Vélez's journey emphasizes resilience and adaptability, with his philosophy: "The journey of an entrepreneur is like climbing a mountain. Enjoy the process, not just the summit" (Forbes, 2020).

Vélez's story illustrates how personal experiences can lead to groundbreaking innovations. By addressing traditional banking's pain points and focusing on customer needs, he transformed Nubank into a fintech giant, setting new standards for banking in Latin America and globally (TechCrunch, 2019).

3.2.3 Character as a Catalyst: The Impact of Strong Founder Traits and the Dynamics of Strong Leadership

We have examined why startup founders with weaknesses or flawed characters caused startup failures and, on the other spectrum, successes with strong character traits. Startups led by founders with strong character traits navigate challenges more effectively. Founders who exhibit authenticity, humility, resilience, and integrity foster a positive company culture, attract top talent, and build stakeholder trust (Sinek, 2009). Authentic leaders inspire their teams by being genuine and transparent, which fosters a sense of loyalty and dedication. Humility allows founders to acknowledge their limitations, seek advice, and collaborate effectively. Resilience enables them to persevere through setbacks and learn from failures, strengthening their resolve and adaptability. Integrity ensures they maintain ethical standards and build long-term trust with investors, customers, and partners.

By embodying these traits, founders create an environment where employees feel valued and motivated, which enhances productivity and innovation. Top talent is drawn to such organizations because they offer a supportive and principled work culture. This reassures founders and leaders that their commitment to strong character traits is beneficial not only for the company's culture but also for attracting the best talent. Additionally, stakeholders, including investors and customers, are more likely to engage with and support a company that operates with transparency and moral integrity.

Sinek (2009) emphasizes that leaders who start with "why" and prioritize purpose over profit create a compelling vision that resonates with people. This approach not only attracts talent but also galvanizes stakeholders around a shared mission, driving collective success. It's a reminder to all leaders that a clear and meaningful purpose can inspire and motivate both internal teams and external stakeholders, leading to collective success. Strong character traits in founders are admirable and essential for sustainable growth and success in the competitive startup landscape.

3.3 Prioritizing People Over Technology: The Right Founder Selection

3.3.1 The Imperative of Startup Founder Selection

The selection process for startup founders should encompass a rigorous evaluation beyond technological prowess. Corporates must assess a founder's ethical stance, vision, and leadership style to ensure a well-rounded fit. While technological skills and innovation are crucial, they are not the sole determinants of a founder's potential for success. A narrow focus on technology alone can miss other critical elements essential for a productive partnership.

The ethical stance of a founder is another critical factor. Ciulla (2004b) underscores that ethics and integrity are at the heart of leadership and significantly impact organizational success (p. 14). A founder's commitment to ethical behavior builds trust with stakeholders, including corporate partners, employees, and customers. Traits such as integrity, resilience, and authenticity reflect a founder's ability to manage setbacks and maintain genuine relationships, which are essential for long-term success (Ciulla, 2004b, p. 56).

A founder's vision is vital for aligning with the corporate entity's long-term goals. This alignment is crucial for ensuring strategic coherence and mutual benefit (Shepherd & DeTienne, 2005, p. 95). Founders with a clear and compelling vision can guide their startups through challenges and opportunities, providing necessary direction and purpose. Additionally, effective leadership is fundamental. Kouzes and Posner (2017) highlight that successful leaders inspire and motivate their teams, fostering a positive work environment that drives innovation and performance. They emphasize that aligning a leader's vision with organizational goals is critical for achieving extraordinary outcomes (p. 38). Evaluating a founder's decision-making skills and ability to manage and inspire their team is essential for predicting their capacity to handle complex situations and sustain progress.

Furthermore, the cultural fit between the founder and the corporate entity is crucial for successful collaboration. Schein (2010) explains that aligning personal and organizational values is essential for harmonious dynamics and effective leadership (p. 68). Understanding how a founder's approach to work and communication fits with the corporate culture helps ensure smooth integration and mutual benefit.

By evaluating these aspects—ethical stance, vision, leadership style—alongside technological prowess, corporate entities can achieve a more comprehensive assessment of a startup founder. This holistic approach will likely result in a better fit between the startup and the corporate entity, leading to smoother integration and more productive collaboration. It considers immediate technological contributions and long-term strategic, cultural, and ethical alignment. Shepherd and DeTienne (2005) support this broader evaluation, noting that personal attributes and potential for financial success are critical to determining a founder's effectiveness and potential (pp. 91–112)

3.3.2 The Approach to Startup Founder Selection

Corporate leaders responsible for open innovation initiatives also act as internal investors. They allocate corporate resources—such as capital, technology, and expertise—to external startups that can bring innovation and competitive advantage to their organization. In this aspect, corporate leaders in open innovation function similarly to startup investors. Just as investors evaluate startups to determine where to allocate their resources, corporate leaders assess startups to decide which ones to collaborate with or invest in. Both roles involve analyzing the startup's potential for success, aligning with strategic goals, and evaluating key founder traits.

Similar Approach Taken by Corporate Leaders and Investors

- **Due Diligence:** Investors conduct thorough due diligence to evaluate a startup's business model, market potential, and team (Collins, 2001, pp. 45–60). Corporate leaders similarly assess startups for strategic fit, technological potential, and compatibility with corporate goals (Goleman, 1995, pp. 82–95).
- **Risk Management:** Investors analyze risks associated with investing in a startup, including market risks, execution risks, and financial risks (Pisano, 2019). Corporate leaders evaluate the risks of collaborating with or investing in a startup, such as integration challenges, technological feasibility, and cultural fit (*Forbes*, 2020, para. 3).
- **Evaluating Founder Traits:** Investors focus on traits like coachability, emotional intelligence, and character to determine a founder's potential for success (Covey, 2004, pp. 101–115). Corporate leaders also prioritize these traits to ensure the startup's leadership can effectively collaborate with the corporate team and drive innovation (Duckworth, 2016, pp. 134–150).

3.3.3 The Criteria for Startup Founder Selection

From the preceding sections, The Imperative Startup Founder Selection, and The Approach to Startup Founder Selection, we conclude to focus and prioritize coachability, emotional intelligence, and character when corporate leaders evaluate their selection of startup founders for open innovations. These traits not only influence the immediate success of the startup but also its long-term sustainability and growth. By focusing on these areas, corporate leaders can identify startup founders with the necessary qualities to navigate the complexities of building and scaling a successful business.

Coachability is accepting feedback, learning from others, and adapting to new information or perspectives. This trait is vital as it demonstrates a founder's willingness to evolve and improve, which is essential in the fast-paced startup environment. In adapting to market changes, coachable founders excel at navigating pivots based on market feedback, making them more agile and responsive to external shifts (*Forbes*, 2021, para. 4). They continuously seek mentorship and apply lessons from others, which is crucial for scaling a business (*Harvard Business Review*, 2016, pp. 30–35). Furthermore, coachable leaders foster a collaborative environment, encouraging input from their team and cultivating a culture of continuous improvement. Ben Silbermann's willingness to listen to feedback and iterate on Pinterest's product based on user input played a pivotal role in the company's success (*Forbes*, 2021, para. 5).

Emotional Intelligence (EI) encompasses the ability to recognize, understand, and manage one's own emotions and the emotions of others. It includes self-awareness, self-regulation, motivation, empathy, and social skills. High EI founders inspire and lead their teams more effectively, fostering loyalty and high performance (Goleman, 1995, pp. 102–110). They handle conflicts adeptly, maintaining a positive and productive work environment (*Harvard Business Review*, 2015, pp. 50–55). Moreover, their strong interpersonal skills enable them to build valuable relationships with investors, partners, and customers. For instance, Tony Hsieh's emphasis on company culture and employee happiness, driven by his high EI, was fundamental to Zappos's success and its acquisition by Amazon (*Harvard Business Review*, 2015, pp. 56–60).

Character encompasses traits such as integrity, authenticity, humility, and resilience. It includes transparency, ethical decision-making, consistency in actions, and overcoming adversity. Integrity builds trust with investors, employees, customers, and other stakeholders (Covey, 2004, pp. 70–80). A founder's character significantly impacts the startup's reputation, which is crucial for long-term success (*Forbes*, 2020, para. 2). Ethical decision-making ensures sustainable business practices and long-term viability.

Warren Buffett's unwavering integrity has earned him immense trust and respect in the investment community (Covey, 2004, pp. 90–95). Yvon Chouinard's focus on integrity and social responsibility has made Patagonia a leader in sustainable business practices (Duckworth, 2016, pp. 140–145).

The three criteria—coachability, emotional intelligence, and character of the startup founders—are also major components of character-based leadership, which we will examine and use in selecting startup founders.

3.3.4 Character-Based Leadership

Character-based leadership emphasizes the leader's personal traits and moral character, highlighting virtues such as integrity, honesty, and courage. Leaders who practice character-based leadership serve as role models by consistently demonstrating ethical behavior and making decisions rooted in a strong moral compass (Northouse, 2018, p. 50). Key elements of this leadership style include integrity, honesty, courage, humility, and empathy. Integrity involves adherence to moral and ethical principles, while honesty requires being truthful and transparent. Courage is essential for taking bold actions in the face of adversity. Humility involves recognizing one's limitations and valuing others' contributions, and empathy is about understanding and sharing the feelings of others.

Character-based leadership also involves a high degree of emotional intelligence. Leaders with emotional intelligence exhibit self-awareness, self-regulation, motivation, empathy, and social skills (Goleman, 1995, p. 45). These traits enhance their ability to connect with others, manage emotions, and navigate social complexities. Self-awareness allows leaders to recognize their feelings and impact on thoughts and behavior, helping them understand their strengths and weaknesses and lead more effectively. Self-regulation involves controlling or redirecting disruptive emotions and impulses, enabling leaders to stay calm under pressure and make thoughtful decisions. Motivation entails harnessing emotions to pursue goals with energy and persistence, inspiring and motivating others. Empathy involves understanding the emotional makeup of others, allowing leaders to build deeper connections and foster a supportive environment. Social skills are essential for managing relationships, helping leaders communicate effectively, resolving conflicts, and leading teams.

Coachability, a crucial aspect of leadership, refers to a leader's willingness to seek feedback, learn from it, and implement necessary changes. It involves openness to new ideas and a continuous desire for self-improvement. A coachable leader demonstrates humility and a commitment to personal growth, aligning with character-based leadership's core tenets. Humility in coachability means recognizing one's limitations and valuing others' contributions, which aligns with character-based leadership's emphasis on humility. By acknowledging that they don't have all the answers, coachable leaders open themselves to learning and growth. Coachable leaders adhere to their moral and ethical principles while being open to constructive criticism, ensuring their development remains grounded in core values.

Empathy is not just a trait but also a crucial element for coachability. Empathetic leaders can better appreciate feedback from their coaches and peers, leading to more meaningful and effective improvements. It takes courage to accept and act on feedback, especially when it involves making significant changes. Coachable leaders demonstrate this courage by taking bold actions to improve and adapt. Being truthful and transparent includes being honest about one's strengths and weaknesses. Coachable leaders are open about their areas for improvement, which facilitates trust and growth.

3.4 Coaching Strategies for Corporate Innovation

Coaching functions as a crucial intermediary in corporate–startup collaborations, ensuring alignment between the startup founder and the corporate innovation manager. Coaches facilitate vision alignment, cultivate mutual understanding, and establish seamless collaboration by mediating between distinct organizational cultures and operational frameworks. Their role minimizes misalignment, mitigates conflicts, and enhances communication effectiveness (Gans et al., 2019, p. 123).

3.4.1 Formulation in Coaching: Structuring the Collaborative Framework

An effective coaching strategy involves formulation, where the coach systematically structures the collaboration by identifying goals, mapping out strategic milestones, and anticipating potential friction points. This structured approach ensures clarity, accountability, and adaptability throughout the partnership. By integrating formulation techniques, coaches guide both parties toward a shared strategic vision, allowing for iterative course corrections when necessary (Clutterbuck, 2010, p. 94).

Formulation in coaching, as outlined by Corrie and Kovacs (2019) and further expanded by Corrie (2024), emphasizes the structured and reflective process through which coaches develop tailored interventions. This method involves assessing both explicit and implicit challenges within the collaboration, ensuring that strategies are continuously refined based on evolving dynamics. By employing formulation, coaches facilitate deeper engagement, nurturing an adaptive framework that enhances problem-solving and strategic alignment. This is crucial in complex open innovation initiatives with corporates collaborating with startups.

3.4.1.1 Aligning Visions and Goals

Coaches facilitate goal-setting exercises where the corporate team and startup founder articulate expectations, priorities, and key success indicators. Through formulation, these elements are synthesized into an actionable road map. This structured process prevents misalignment, ensuring that all stakeholders work toward a unified objective (Gans et al., 2019, p. 145).

3.4.1.2 Building Mutual Understanding

Successful collaboration requires trust and open dialogue. Coaches cultivate this by structuring communication frameworks, such as regular check-ins, retrospective reviews, and transparent feedback mechanisms. This process fosters psychological safety, allowing both parties to discuss concerns candidly and refine collaboration dynamics continuously (Sinek, 2009, p. 78).

3.4.1.3 Preempting and Addressing Potential Issues

Coaches leverage formulation to proactively identify potential roadblocks. By maintaining consistent engagement with both teams, they detect early signs of miscommunication or conflicting expectations. If a startup struggles with a corporate partner's rigid structures, the coach facilitates recalibration discussions, ensuring expectations remain realistic and productive (Gans et al., 2019, p. 160).

3.4.1.4 Strategizing for Sustainable Collaboration

Beyond troubleshooting, coaches employ formulation to design long-term collaboration frameworks. To enhance synergy, they integrate tailored solutions, such as cross-cultural training or joint team-building initiatives. The ultimate goal is to cultivate an adaptive, resilient partnership rather than a transactional engagement (Sinek, 2009, p. 92).

3.4.2 The Coaching Approach

A structured and analytical approach is essential to developing an effective coaching strategy for selecting startup founders based on character-based leadership. This process includes:

1   **Assessing Organizational Needs and Goals:** Conducting a needs assessment to determine leadership priorities in open innovation (Goleman, 2000, p. 45).
2   **Understanding the Target Audience:** Evaluating corporate leaders' competencies and perspectives on character-based leadership (Heifetz & Linsky, 2002, p. 78).
3   **Aligning with Organizational Culture:** Ensuring coaching strategies resonate with corporate values and operational processes (Schein, 2010, p. 128).
4   **Leveraging Existing Resources:** Incorporating established leadership frameworks into the coaching process (Bennis, 2009, p. 65).
5   **Piloting and Iterating:** Testing strategies through small-scale initiatives before full-scale implementation (Kouzes & Posner, 2012, p. 94).
6   **Providing Continuous Support:** Offering sustained coaching, resources, and guidance to corporate leaders as they refine their founder selection criteria (Heifetz & Linsky, 2002, p. 102).

3.4.3 Coaching Strategies for Assessing Character-Based Leadership in Startup Founders

Identifying startup founders who exhibit character-based leadership is essential for building successful corporate–startup collaborations. Corporate leaders must assess founders' integrity, resilience, and empathy using structured methodologies. The following are practical tools and approaches to evaluate and select founders with strong leadership potential, fostering successful partnerships in corporate–startup collaborations:

1   **Character Strengths Assessment:** Tools such as the VIA Character Strengths Survey (Peterson & Seligman, 2004) and CliftonStrengths (Clifton et al., 2006a) evaluate essential leadership attributes. Corporate leaders can participate in training sessions on interpreting these assessments for informed decision-making (Peterson & Seligman, 2004, p. 36; Clifton et al., 2006a, p. 45).
2   **Behavioral Interview Techniques:** Conducting structured interviews that probe past experiences to gauge leadership capabilities (Korn Ferry, 2014, p. 22). Utilizing role-playing exercises to refine corporate leaders' ability to assess responses effectively.
3   **Leadership Simulation Exercises:** Developing real-world scenarios where founders demonstrate their problem-solving and decision-making skills under pressure (Hogan & Kaiser, 2005, p. 172). Structuring these simulations to mirror challenges specific to corporate innovation programs.
4   **Values Alignment Workshops:** Conducting sessions where corporate leaders articulate their company's values and assess alignment with potential startup founders (Schein, 2010, p. 128). Employing discussion groups and value-mapping exercises to ensure coherence between corporate and startup ethos.
5   **Peer and 360-Degree Feedback:** Gathering insights from colleagues, subordinates, and advisors to construct a comprehensive leadership profile (Kouzes & Posner, 2012, p. 94). Equipping corporate leaders with analytical tools to interpret multisource feedback effectively.
6   **Case Study Analysis:** Reviewing case studies of successful and unsuccessful startup founders to derive lessons on leadership characteristics (Finkelstein et al., 2009, p. 58), and facilitating structured discussions where corporate leaders draw parallels to their own selection criteria.

By embedding formulation into the coaching framework, corporate leaders develop structured, evidence-based approaches to selecting startup founders. This ensures partnerships are built on character-based leadership, aligning with long-term innovation objectives.

3.5 Crafting Effective Coaching Strategies: An Example

Understanding the utmost importance of character-based leadership is crucial for corporate leaders tasked with selecting startup founders in open innovation initiatives. These leaders often bring expertise in evaluating business models and market potential but may lack the necessary skills to assess the ethical dimensions that define effective startup founders with the right character. The following scenario provides a practical example of how coaching can bridge this gap, empowering leaders to refine their approach and make more informed decisions when selecting startup partners.

3.5.1 Case Study: Coaching Strategy Integrating Character-Based Leadership and Personalization in Founder Selection

Scenario Overview

Sarah, a corporate leader managing her organization's open innovation initiative, has built her expertise on assessing business models and market potential. However, her professional success in traditional business practices contrasts with a significant gap: an inability to evaluate character-based leadership traits and emotional intelligence (EI). These competencies, pivotal in identifying startup founders aligned with organizational culture, remain absent from her current selection framework. Sarah seeks to refine her evaluation process to incorporate these human-centered factors, recognizing their importance in achieving effective collaboration and long-term innovation success.

A personalized coaching session was conducted to address Sarah's challenge, using the Formulation of Coaching framework to craft a strategic, individualized approach. This framework—rooted in problem definition, hypothesis generation, intervention design, and evaluation—provided the structural rigor needed for meaningful progress (Corrie & Kovacs, 2019, p. 34).

Formulation Framework: Structuring the Coaching Session

1 Problem Definition

> The coaching session began with an in-depth discussion of Sarah's current challenges. She acknowledged her reliance on quantitative criteria, such as market viability and scalability, while overlooking qualitative dimensions, such as leadership integrity and team compatibility.
>
> The coach identified the central issue: Sarah's framework lacked the tools and strategies to evaluate a founder's ability to build trust, inspire collaboration, and demonstrate resilience under pressure. The absence of these considerations jeopardized the potential for effective partnerships and undermined the organization's open innovation goals.

COACH'S REFLECTION: "By prioritizing technical and financial metrics, Sarah inadvertently marginalized the human element of collaboration. This imbalance compromises the integrity and cohesion required for successful innovation."

(Corrie & Kovacs, 2019, p. 38).

2 Hypothesis Generation

The coach posited that integrating character-based leadership and emotional intelligence assessments into Sarah's evaluation process would improve her ability to select founders who could cultivate trust, manage conflicts, and adapt to complex challenges. These traits are essential for navigating the nuanced dynamics of corporate–startup partnerships

(Lane, Corrie, & Kovacs, 2025, p. 44).

This hypothesis included personalization as a cornerstone, tailoring the evaluation process to align with Sarah's analytical strengths and the organization's specific cultural and operational needs.

COACH'S HYPOTHESIS: "Personalizing the framework will empower Sarah to systematically assess leadership character and interpersonal competencies, thereby ensuring alignment with both corporate goals and team dynamics."

(Corrie & Kovacs, 2019, p. 56).

3 Intervention Design

The intervention focused on equipping Sarah with practical tools and strategies to operationalize the hypothesis. The coach emphasized personalization, recommending methods aligned with Sarah's structured thinking and professional expertise.

Coaching Dialogue:

COACH: "Sarah, we need to refine your selection process to assess not just technical expertise but also the human qualities that drive sustainable collaboration. Let's focus on character-based leadership and emotional intelligence. What challenges do you anticipate in applying these concepts?"

SARAH: "I'm unsure how to quantify traits like integrity and resilience. My current approach focuses on measurable outcomes, and I'm not familiar with tools for evaluating these softer skills."

COACH: "That's an excellent starting point. Let's explore tools and methods tailored to your analytical strengths while addressing these qualitative factors. For instance, we can use structured behavioral interviews to gauge past actions that reflect core character traits like trustworthiness and empathy."

Proposed Methods:

1   **Behavioral Interviews With Tailored Questions**: Develop specific questions such as:

   • "Describe a time you rebuilt trust after a disagreement. What steps did you take?"

- "Can you share an example of leading a team through a period of uncertainty?"
- These questions provide insights into past behaviors, highlighting how candidates navigate interpersonal challenges (Korn Ferry, 2014, p. 47).

2   **Leadership Simulation Exercises**: Design realistic scenarios to observe how candidates handle stress, mediate conflicts, and collaborate under pressure (Hogan & Kaiser, 2005, p. 62).

3   **Emotional Intelligence Assessments**: Introduce validated tools like the Emotional and Social Competency Inventory (ESCI) to measure empathy, adaptability, and self-awareness (Goleman et al., 2002, p. 108).

4   **Values-Alignment Workshops**: Facilitate discussions to evaluate how the candidate's values align with the company's mission and culture (Schein, 2010, p. 88).

5   **Feedback from 360-Degree Reviews**: Collect input from peers, subordinates, and supervisors to gain a comprehensive understanding of the candidate's leadership character and interpersonal impact (Kouzes & Posner, 2012, p. 88).

COACH: "These methods create a holistic view of the candidate, integrating measurable outcomes with nuanced human factors. This approach aligns with your preference for structured, actionable processes."

4 Evaluation

The coach and Sarah established criteria to evaluate the success of the revised framework:

- **Improved Founder Alignment**: Assess the extent to which selected founders embody the organization's values and drive team cohesion.
- **Enhanced Decision-Making Confidence**: Monitor Sarah's confidence in applying the framework and using the new tools.
- **Collaboration Outcomes**: Measure the impact of the selected founders on project efficiency and team morale (Lane et al., 2025, p. 72).

Outcomes and Insights

The personalized formulation approach transformed Sarah's selection process, equipping her with a robust framework to evaluate character-based leadership and emotional intelligence. Founders selected using the new criteria demonstrated more substantial alignment with organizational culture and significantly enhanced team dynamics.

Coach's Reflection

"The incorporation of personalized strategies enabled Sarah to transcend traditional evaluation metrics and embrace a more holistic, human-centered approach. This transformation underscores the power of tailoring interventions to the unique context of the coachee and the organization" (Corrie & Kovacs, 2019, p. 62).

Discussion Questions

1   **Assessing Leadership Beyond Metrics:** Sarah initially relied on quantitative evaluation methods, but leadership success depends on intangible qualities like integrity and resilience. How can corporate leaders balance quantitative and qualitative assessments when selecting startup founders?
2   **Integrating Emotional Intelligence Into Selection Processes:** The case study introduces structured tools like behavioral interviews and 360-degree feedback to evaluate emotional intelligence. How can organizations ensure these assessments are objective and aligned with business outcomes?
3   **Character-Based Leadership in High-Stakes Environments:** Trust, adaptability, and collaboration are critical in corporate–startup partnerships. What are the risks of selecting a technically proficient founder who lacks these traits? How have failed collaborations demonstrated the consequences of overlooking leadership character?
4   **Challenges in Measuring "Soft" Leadership Qualities:** Sarah struggled with quantifying traits such as empathy and resilience. How can corporate innovation teams develop reliable indicators for evaluating these attributes during the selection process?
5   **Customization of Coaching Strategies:** The case study highlights a personalized coaching approach tailored to Sarah's analytical strengths. How can coaches adapt their frameworks to accommodate different leadership styles and corporate cultures?
6   **Long-Term Impact of Founder Selection on Innovation Success:** A mismatch between a startup founder and a corporate partner can lead to misalignment in vision and execution. How can companies track and evaluate the long-term success of founders selected through character-based and emotional intelligence assessments?

Conclusion

A structured and personalized approach to founder selection strengthens corporate–startup collaborations by ensuring alignment between leadership character and organizational values. The Formulation in Coaching framework provided the necessary structure, enabling Sarah to systematically integrate character-based leadership and emotional intelligence assessments into her evaluation process. This strategic refinement enhanced her ability to identify founders who cultivate trust, navigate interpersonal challenges, and adapt to complex environments. Emotional intelligence emerged as a decisive factor, differentiating leaders who promote team collaboration and resilience. A holistic evaluation framework that blends structured assessments with qualitative insights allows for a more accurate appraisal of leadership potential. By adopting a tailored methodology, Sarah improved her decision-making process, reinforcing the value of a human-centered, strategic approach in corporate innovation.

Conclusion

In corporate innovation, the importance of the founder's character cannot be overstated. *While technology remains an essential component*, it is often the founder's attributes that determine the success or failure of a corporate–startup collaboration. Selecting founders with integrity, emotional intelligence, adaptability, and a clear vision aligns startups and corporate partners in a way that technological compatibility alone cannot achieve. This chapter underscores that, in any partnership, who the founder is often matters as much as the technology they bring.

Corporate leaders engaged in open innovation learn that prioritizing character-based leadership traits in founders can lead to more productive and sustainable collaborations. For example, selecting a founder who displays resilience ensures the partnership has a leader who can endure setbacks, adapt to new challenges, and respond flexibly—qualities that are critical in today's unpredictable business landscape. Similarly, a founder with high emotional intelligence will build stronger connections within the corporate environment, navigating potential conflicts and establishing trust with stakeholders, employees, and partners.

This focus on the human element within corporate–startup partnerships moves the emphasis from a purely technology-driven approach to one centered on leadership, authenticity, and integrity. Traits such as these help to build a culture of transparency and accountability, reducing the risk of ethical lapses or misalignments that have led to high-profile failures. Cases like Theranos exemplify the hazards of overlooking character, demonstrating that even the most groundbreaking technology can become irrelevant if the founder lacks transparency and ethical grounding.

Coaching emerges as a vital intermediary in helping corporations identify and nurture these essential traits in startup founders. By guiding leaders to assess potential partners beyond technical capabilities, coaching facilitates a more comprehensive and sustainable approach to collaboration. Through a combination of values alignment, behavioral insights, and continuous feedback, coaches help corporates understand what to look for in a founder and how to foster those qualities for long-term success.

In conclusion, success in corporate innovation hinges on aligning the right people, not just the right technology. By championing a founder's character and values, corporate leaders position their organizations to benefit from partnerships that are not only innovative but also built to last. Emphasizing character-first selection creates a foundation where technology serves as a powerful tool, but people drive progress, resilience, and integrity within the collaboration.

References

Clutterbuck, D. (2014). *Coaching the team at work*. Nicholas Brealey Publishing.

Goleman, D., Boyatzis, R., & McKee, A. (2013). *Primal leadership: Unleashing the power of emotional intelligence*. Harvard Business Review Press.

Hogan, R., & Kaiser, R. B. (2005). *What we know about leadership*. *Review of General Psychology*, 9(2), 169–180.

Korn Ferry. (2014). *Leadership architect competency library*. Korn Ferry Institute.

Schein, E. H. (2010). *Organizational culture and leadership* (4th ed.). Jossey-Bass.

Chapter 4

Shared Vision, Shared Dreams

In today's rapidly evolving business landscape, collaboration between corporates and startups has become essential to drive innovation and maintain a competitive edge. Chapter 4, "Shared Vision, Shared Dreams," explores the pivotal role of a shared vision in corporate–startup partnerships. A powerful, collective vision not only serves as the strategic guide that keeps both entities aligned, fostering synergy and purpose throughout the collaboration, but also leads to increased innovation, better problem-solving, and a more resilient partnership. For corporates, vision often evolves within established frameworks, while for startups, it embodies the founders' aspirations to create something transformative from the ground up. This chapter delves into how differing motivations and organizational cultures can create challenges in achieving alignment, underscoring the need for a deliberate approach to cocreate a shared vision.

A shared vision within corporate–startup partnerships is more than a statement of intent; it is a cohesive force that aligns goals, nurtures trust, and drives collective action. The corporate perspective brings experience, scale, and structure, while startups inject agility, innovative ideas, and fresh approaches. When these forces unite under a shared vision, they can overcome structural and cultural differences to create a formidable team. Through practical frameworks, real-world examples, and leadership insights, this chapter provides tools for coaches and leaders to guide both corporate and startup teams toward establishing a collaborative vision—one that leverages each partner's strengths to fulfil shared goals and dreams.

Key Takeaways

- **Vision as Strategic Guidance**: Vision operates as the North Star for organizations, setting a clear strategic path during volatile market conditions. A well-crafted vision allows companies to navigate challenges with purpose and resolve.
- **Dual Components of Vision**: Effective visions consist of core ideology and an envisioned future. The core ideology captures the company's enduring

DOI: 10.4324/9781003469155-6

values, while the envisioned future outlines ambitious, achievable goals that inspire and energize teams.

- **Difference in Vision Development**: Corporate visions often evolve from existing frameworks to adapt to market changes. However, startups build vision from scratch, representing the founder's drive and aspirations to create something transformative.
- **Vision in Startups—the Seed of Innovation**: Innovation is inherently tied to a startup's vision. Startups are formed around unique ideas that promise to solve a problem, often leveraging cutting-edge technologies to create products that disrupt existing markets.
- **Design Thinking for Ideation**: The design thinking approach facilitates startup ideation by focusing on empathy and user-centered design. This framework promotes innovative, practical solutions that align the product with user needs.
- **Leadership's Role in Visioning**: Visioning demands active leadership, where leaders communicate an aspirational direction and secure commitment from their teams. Leaders create alignment around the vision and inspire teams to work toward shared objectives.
- **Communication and Persuasion**: Effective communication is fundamental to gaining stakeholder buy-in. Leaders who excel in communication can inspire commitment to the vision by addressing shared values and mutual goals.
- **Vision Alignment as a Collaboration Challenge**: Corporate–startup collaborations often encounter difficulties in aligning visions due to contrasting motivations. Successful collaborations require intentional efforts to cocreate a shared vision that respects corporate objectives and the startup's innovative spirit.
- **Case Study of Vision Loyalty**: Craig Silverstein and Google's example demonstrates how shared beliefs and alignment with a company's mission can cultivate lasting commitment. This commitment is cultivated by a deeply resonant vision that aligns with personal values.
- **Importance of Shared Purpose**: Focusing on a shared purpose provides a stable foundation for collaborations. When corporate and startup connect on a shared "why?," it drives engagement and aligns both parties toward common goals.
- **Medium-Term Vision**: Establishing a medium-term outlook, usually around three years, helps both corporates and startups manage resources, adapt strategies, and stay focused on achieving milestones essential for sustained collaboration success.
- **From Collective Purpose to Collective Goals**: Translating vision into actionable goals is essential for collaborations between diverse entities. Establishing collective goals ensures both parties are aligned in their approach to achieving the vision.
- **Defining Goals Through SMART Objectives**: Specific, measurable, achievable, relevant, and time-bound (SMART) goals enable teams to progress

systematically toward the vision, providing structure and accountability to collaborative efforts.

- **Clarity on Strategy and Tactics**: Strategy and tactics provide the practical road map for achieving the vision. A successful strategy considers the mission and purpose while avoiding the allure of technology-led directions that may sidetrack teams.
- **Maintaining Alignment Through Change**: Corporate and startup teams must be agile in a rapidly evolving landscape. However, staying true to the shared vision and purpose enables consistent alignment, even as tactical adjustments are made to adapt to new developments.

4.1 Vision Is Often Seen as the North Star

Vision is often seen as the North Star that guides an organization or the belief system that underpins the organization's trajectory, especially during a period of uncertainty in the market. It is the blueprint that will allow the organization to navigate the vicissitudes of the market with clarity and confidence. Nanus (1992) states, "An attractive, worthwhile, achievable, and widely shared vision of the future is the most powerful engine driving an organisation toward excellence and long-range success."

Naturally, the next question we must ask ourselves is, "What is a vision, especially an organization's vision?"

Carton et al. (2014b) describe organizational vision as having qualities of being idealized. Vision is seen as a perfect or an aspirational state the organization aims to achieve. This gives the relevant stakeholders "clear objectives, sense of direction, priority, holistic consideration, coordinated actions and the basis of performance measures" (Su, Wang, et al., 2004). While some may argue that a vision, with its ideal state qualities, can pose a challenge in its realization, it nonetheless serves as a strategic intent of the organization. Businesses will be able to look to this true north as a form of immutable guide to steer their strategic decision-making.

A well-conceived vision is defined as consisting of two major components: core ideology and envisioned future (Collins & Porras, 1996). Core ideology represents the foundation of the organization's existence, while the envisioned future embodies its aspirations and the direction it desires to pursue.

In core ideology, the organization will find the enduring raison d'être that will guide its growth, enduring the changes brought by the passing of times, such as the change of leadership and the advancement of technologies. It will always be the true north that will guide future leaders to stay true to the foundation of its existence. The embedded wisdom will also fuel the culture of the company, the collective wisdom of the group, shaped partly by "a set of structures, routines, rules and norms" (Schein, 2004). This culture then enables the organization to effectively respond to the challenges posed by its operating environment.

Collins and Porras (1996) further defined the subcomponents of core ideology and envisioned the future as follows:

1   Core Ideology

- Core Values: Essential tenets of the organization, guiding principles to those in the organization that are not time bound.
- Core Purpose: The soul of the organization, the reason for being of the organization.

2   Envisioned Future

- Big, Hairy, Audacious Goals (BHAGs): Compelling, clear, and challenging goals that energize and inspire the team. These goals are simultaneously easy to understand and attention-grabbing.
- Vivid Description: Translating the words into images and projecting these images into the employees' minds. This will essentially create an image in their minds that they will constantly carry with them.

Mishe (2000a) also describes six essential qualities that define an effective vision:

- Vision communicates a sense of direction.
- Vision establishes the context to operate the company.
- Vision describes a future condition.
- Vision motivates people.
- Vision inspires employees to work toward a common state or set of goals.
- Vision serves as a central point of an organization's behavior and performance, including the development of strategy and its measurement to attain the set of goals.

The evidence provided by both these researchers consistently showed that a well-defined vision is pivotal to the organization's future performance. Henceforth, critical care must be taken in the choice of words, as a well-defined vision statement must answer the question, "What do we want to become?" (Djordjevic, 2021a).

Furthermore, the choice of words must convey these four generic features (Nutt and Backoff, 1997) for the vision to be effective in enhancing organizational performance. They are:

1   **Possibility:** It should empower the possibility for a dramatic organizational performance.
2   **Desirability:** It should draw upon shared organizational practices and values on how things are done.

3 **Actionability:** It should motivate employees to take actions that are relevant to them.
4 **Articulation:** It should possess an image that can be projected in the minds of the employees to communicate the organization's trajectory.

4.1.1 Vision Development in Corporate Versus Startups

Vision development can be a lengthy affair that involves collaborative engagement among the leadership team. Here, the leaders are expected to represent the employees under their care and contribute to the vision.

It is also an iterative refinement process. This process is often led by an external consultant or coach to help the leadership team, especially the chief executive officer, craft a vision that is aligned with the strategic goals of the organization.

Although there is no clear evidence that vision development in large corporations, especially public-listed ones, is affected by quarterly earnings reporting to shareholders, it inevitably may have somewhat affected the CEO when they are drawing up their vision for the business.

Moreover, most corporates are not specifically developing a new vision but, in fact, are revising their existing vision to be congruent with the passing of time and changes in their offerings. While on the one hand, corporates can benefit from being guided by their experience and wisdom from the past, the vision development process may be less transformative than a new startup, which is crafting its core identity and future direction for the first time.

Meanwhile, on the other hand, startups are truly creating a vision from the very beginning, calling into being a future that has yet to be. Bill Aulet (2024), the author of *Disciplined Entrepreneurship. 24 Steps to a Successful Startup*, described the following three most common ways to start a new venture:

1 **Idea:** Thinking of a new idea that can change the world, no matter how small, in a positive way.
2 **Technology:** Capitalizing on a breakthrough technology and deploying that technology to the market to have a positive impact on the world. The startup founder need not necessarily be the inventor of that technology.
3 **Passion:** A belief that startup and entrepreneurship are the most effective ways to bring about positive change in the world. Passion is the answer to the question, "Why are you starting a company, or why are you an entrepreneur?" Passion is also the reason that would sustain and motivate startup founders through difficult times. Although the activity, the core of entrepreneurship, is about making money, pursuing money is not considered a passion. Entrepreneurship is seen as "an ethical activity to make the world a better place, which is not simply profiteering" (Brad Feld, as cited in Aulet, 2024, pg. 3).

Aulet (2024) further suggested that one can derive ideas and technology from passion. From passion, a startup founder could generate ideas from problems faced by the market or even from personal experiences. The key question to ask is, "What problem am I solving today?"

On the technology front, generative AI, metaverse, and blockchain could offer the push that would encourage startup founders to create inventive solutions with the technology. The key is to productize the technology into a solution or product to solve a client's problem.

The most significant difference between a corporate and a startup in vision development is clear. For a corporate, the vision-setting process is often an activity undertaken to satisfy the expectations of multiple shareholders. In a public-listed corporation, shareholders could range from corporates to a multitude of individuals. In contrast, the vision is raison d'être—the fundamental purpose and driving force of a single individual, the founder.

Herein lies the biggest challenge in a corporate–startup collaboration: Vision development is derived from different motivations. One is almost an institutional activity, while the other is a very personal activity whereby the individual is wholly invested in realizing the vision, often with their own money and resources. In short, for the collaboration to be successful, there must be a deliberate effort to cocreate a vision that matches both the motivation of the corporate team and that of the founder.

4.1.2 An Observation: Innovation Is Inherent in a Startup's Vision

Guy Kawasaki, a famous venture capitalist and startup evangelist, in his book, *The Art of the Start*, describes a startup role as "alleviating pain or providing pleasure" to an existing problem. He further added that each startup must have a "secret sauce" to achieve the desired result of alleviating pain or providing pleasure. In short, the "secret sauce" is the innovation that is expected of a startup that will enable it to be deemed valuable for investment.

All startups begin with an idea—an innovative idea. In fact, the first process that must take place prior to forming a startup entity is the "ideation process." Would-be startup founders will be given a problem with a substantial market size to brainstorm on. The outcome of these brainstorming sessions will hopefully be a set of innovative ideas that show potential to be productized or commercialized.

To facilitate a structured manner of brainstorming that could help birth a product or solution that can, in Kawasaki's words, "alleviate pain and provide pleasure," the most popular framework that is used in the startup world is the "design thinking approach." David Kelley and Tim Brown, founders of IDEO, are widely credited with inventing the term "design thinking" and developing a framework that places great importance on empathy, iteration and user-centered design (Falvo et al., 2023b).

The beauty of the design thinking approach is that it begins with a focus on empathizing with the potential user of the product or solution. This helps create a product that is relevant to the market; there are potential users who will be willing to pay for it.

A typical design thinking approach, according to the article "What Is Design Thinking & What Is It Important?" by Han (2022) of the Harvard Business School, consist of four phases:

1   **Clarify**: The key here is to identify the problem statement before devising the most suitable solution. Approaches that can be adopted include literature reviews, practical observation, interviews, and more.
2   **Ideate**: With clarity of the problem that needs to be solved, ideation is where creativity in using technology or the simple introduction of new processes can be introduced. The key is to create an innovative solution that resolves the problem and is hopefully repeatable. This stage can be an iterative process until the best solution is found.
3   **Develop**: This stage involves prototyping, testing, and, above all, experimenting until a conceptual design emerges from a range of possible solutions derived from the ideate stage.
4   **Implement**: This stage is the final production of the solution, which involves work such as testing, reworking the design, reiterating, and retesting until a solution is found. Similar to the ideate stage, this also can be an iterative process.

4.1.3 Visioning as an Act of Leadership

"Effective leaders adopt challenging new visions of what is both possible and desirable, communicate their visions, and persuade others to become so committed to these new directions that they are eager to lend their resources and energies to make them happen" (Nanus, 1992).

It is the leader's role of any organization, especially a startup, to adopt challenging new visions. It must be a future-oriented goal that is first possible with available resources or technology but also "desirable." We can safely assume that the desirability of this new vision is an acquiescence of the wishes of the stakeholders unique to a particular organization. These stakeholders could be internal and external, such as internal and external employees and customers, who are external.

The leader's prerogative is to balance the "desirability" of the organization's stakeholders with the possibility of executing the vision. Hence, the success of any vision hinges on the leader's ability to assess the organization's resources and capabilities realistically. Effective leaders must adopt a strategic approach involving an overarching vision that spans a longer period while breaking down the vision into SMART goals: specific, measurable, achievable, realistic and time-bound (Doran, 1981). Studies have suggested that effective leaders are able to translate their vision into specific, achievable goals, thereby mobilizing their organization towards a common goal (Skok, 2024).

These goals will act as crucial guideposts and checkpoints, providing the organization with a clear framework to navigate its strategic journey to the desired vision as they are systematically achieved. This is helpful for both a large organization and a startup as it encapsulates objective measurements that will allow leaders to make decisions that reflect reality on the ground. Moreover, the ability to make critical decision-making at a critical inflection point, known as "pivoting" in startups, can make or break the startup. Facebook pivoted from a college students–only service of posting photographs of themselves or their clubs to a social media platform that has changed the fate of nations and, subsequently, millions of lives.

SMART goals also can serve as a checklist on the resources and energies needed to achieve the vision. The approach will help organizations first identify potential obstacles and then work with available resources to overcome them. This is also an opportunity for stakeholders, labeled as "others" by Nanus (1992), to know when and how to lend their resources and energies to bring the leader's vision to pass. It is also an opportunity for the transformative power of innovation to be brought forward through the collaborative power of all these stakeholders.

Engaging stakeholders in understanding what is required of them may represent the least challenging aspect of effective leadership in shaping the organization's vision. Vision alone is insufficient; it is the securing of their dedication and commitment that drives the organization forward in realizing its goals and, subsequently, its vision. This is especially true in a startup where the financial ability to procure these commitments is almost non-existent. Effective communication plays and will continue to play a pivotal in this process.

Succinctly, communication is the fundamental skill for persuading various stakeholders, such as employees, customers, investors, and even vendors, to commit to the vision. It is an attempt to persuade, to cajole, others to lend not only their energies but also resources to aid the achievement of the vision.

What are communication skills, and how much bearing does it have on the ability to persuade? Tian, Logendran, and Mariappan (2023) defined communication skills as "exchanging ideas, attitudes, facts, and points of view with another person" and found that communication skills have a direct bearing on how persuasive one can be. The quantitative evaluation of their research was an objective observation of the purchasing behavior of the customer: Did the customer buy after being persuaded by the salesperson with good to excellent communication skills? Drawing parallels to the example, a leader of an organization can be considered persuasive if stakeholders buy into the vision and begin to spend their energies and resources to build the vision.

According to Tian, Logendran, and Mariappan (2023) the key to persuasion lies in effect on having a dialogue in four major areas:

1 **Ideas:** To allow the flow of ideas to go back and forth.
2 **Attitudes:** To be able to receive others' attitudes and simultaneously project one's own attitude.
3 **Facts:** A conversation revolving around facts to "ground the argument."
4 **Points of View:** To see each other's point of view, to truly put one into the shoes of another, and to see his point of view.

If and when a leader is able to create this exchange of ideas, attitudes, facts, and points of view and yet still retain the vision that was first conceived, sometimes with a few adjustments, incorporating ideas that were birthed out of the exchanges, the leader can effectively gain commitment from stakeholders.

A case in point is the story of Craig Silverstein, Google Employee Number 3, after the cofounders Larry Page and Sergey Brin.

4.1.4 Case Study: Commitment to a Vision

The excerpt below is from a previous work by the authors, *Department of Startup. Why Every Fortune 500 Should Have One* (Lee & Yong, 2019).

Craig Silverstein was Google Employee Number 3, after the co-founders Larry Page and Sergey Brin. He was the first person employed by Page and Brin after having studied together with them at Stanford University for his PhD. Silverstein's contribution to the building blocks of Google is legendary amongst Google. In Page's own words, Silverstein's codes were instrumental in the success of Google today. A Harvard graduate as well, he was also admitted to the Phi Beta Kappa, the oldest and most prestigious honour society in America, honouring outstanding liberal arts and science students. He had plenty of choices to work with the top one per cent of the Fortune 500, but instead, he chose to trust his fellow students, Larry Page, Sergey Brin, and Google.

What drove Silverstein to put his trust in Google and its founders so early in the startup phase? Google was just an idea in a dorm room in the halls of Stanford at that time.

The answer was crystal clear in Silverstein's goodbye e-mail to the staff in Google when he left in the year 2012 to join Khan Academy. Silverstein had this to say for his 13 years at Google,

"While a lot has changed at Google over the years, I think we've done a remarkable job of staying true to our core mission of making the world a better place by making information more accessible and useful. I am looking forward to pursuing that same mission, though in a slightly different way, at Khan."

Craig Silverstein trusted Google, Larry Page, and Sergey Brin, and their belief system matches his—to make the world a better place by making information accessible and useful. Google and its founder reciprocated that trust and stayed true to their values and belief system. In his final parting words, Silverstein again emphasised how Google's belief system had affected him to choose Google, and he wrote, "When I write my massive 4-volume autobiography, "Craig Silverstein: the Man Behind the Legend," I will devote an entire volume to my years at Google. I can't emphasise enough how meaningful my time at Google has been, and how meaningful all of you have been to it."

Throughout his time with Google, Silverstein continued to be committed to the vision set forth by Larry and Sergey and was seen by many as the third founder. From his tenure with Google, Silverstein amassed a total of US$950 million in remuneration.

Questions to Ponder

1   The bond that Silverstein shared with Larry and Sergey at Stanford may have been instrumental in persuading him to commit to Google's vision and belief system. What other communication styles can convince Silverstein if you were Larry and Sergey?

2   Silverstein could have worked with any of the world's top 1% companies upon his graduation, but he chose to commit his energy and resources to a fledgling startup. How do you convince your stakeholders to commit to a promise in the form of a vision versus the immediate rewards available to them in the present? Would words suffice?

3   Silverstein was convinced that he had spent meaningful time in Google to the point that he would dedicate an entire volume to his massive to-be-written four-volume autobiography. What is your thought on helping your stakeholders spend meaningful time in your organization?

4   How can you help your stakeholders relate their meaningful time in your organization to the vision that you are espousing to them? Could their "meaningful time" be a personal vision that sits under the umbrella of the organization's vision?

Now, if leaders can communicate the vision to their teams, are they able to communicate it to another team that does not share their DNA or culture? This is a classic problem with corporates and startups. They do not share the same DNA and have a different culture in how they meet and overcome challenges.

Corporates have made the mistake of turning their offices into a semi-playground filled with Ping-Pong tables and video games to attract and to help create the environment necessary for both teams to work together. Some had chosen to move their team to a coworking space where the startups are. Although commendable, these efforts are nothing beyond a window dressing exercise. Both teams, corporate and startups, must work to find common ground and a common vision and then communicate that shared vision to both teams. This then begets the question: How should they go about it, or even more specifically, who should lead this search for a common ground?

Theoretically, it should be a joint effort where both corporates and startups are partners-of-equal. But in reality, that is not the case. As of the time of writing, almost all corporate–startup collaboration programs are funded by corporates, where startups are invited to pitch their solution to the corporates. The authors of this book have yet to witness a corporate–startup innovation program that is led by startup, where corporates are being selected.

Notwithstanding, if there is a strong founder or a startup with a strong technology, the narrative could change in favor of the startup. Nonetheless, these are very few and in between.

The solution is an introduction of a coach that could facilitate the conversation necessary to create a more balanced relationship, and to strive to create a team of equals by focusing on what the authors term as "shared purpose and shared motivation."

4.2 Shared Purpose and Shared Motivation

Today, in a typical corporate innovation collaboration, the partnership is likely anchored on the technology offered by the startup. The corporate is likely to see the potential of that technology in helping it fulfil its vision or stay ahead of competitors. The technology is also likely to be seen as the "trump card" that could disrupt the industry that they are in.

The startup, on the other hand, is subservient to the corporate demand as it is, in its nature, cash-hungry and lacking in resources in many ways. This includes talents to continue to drive innovation and help bring the innovation in the form of a minimum-value product (MVP) to the market. All these are abundant in the counterpart that the startup is trying to collaborate with, the corporate.

In a relationship where the dynamics are dictated by a resource-rich counterpart, such as the corporate, the likelihood of creating an equal partnership with a shared vision is almost nonexistent. However, that does not mean that it is impossible.

The key is to focus on the search of a collective purpose. In David Clutterbuck's definitive guide to team coaching, *Coaching the Team at Work* (2020), he defines "collective purpose" as the foundation of the team culture. He further describes some of the notable characteristics of collective purpose as follows:

- A connection of each member's instincts and what is meaningful and worthwhile
- A connection with each member's personal purpose
- A shared "narrative of rightness"—a collection of stories of members that illustrate the purpose

One key method for discovering collective purpose is through reflection. The team conducts reflective dialogue, making it explicit among the members. By making it explicit, every member of the team will be able to channel their motivation to achieve it, giving it power.

If shared vision is an aspiration of a desired new future shared by both the corporate and the startup, collective purpose would be the "why" to that future. Hence, the path to a shared vision is the discovery of the shared "why." Both parties must find the reason as to why they are collaborating, especially in meeting their medium-term "why." A medium-term outlook of no more than three years is a good rule of thumb for several reasons, as follows:

- The startup will likely be "burning cash" and needs to raise new investments. The collaboration must yield at least a "proof-of-concept" or better, a "minimum viable product (MVP) that could already be introduced to the market" to increase the startup's prospects of attracting new investors.
- The corporate could use medium-term planning to adapt to the industry's changing circumstances and manage resources effectively to bring the collaboration to success.
- The speed of change in the technology scene could also render the initial innovation or solution obsolete. This is a good opportunity to examine whether there is a need to pivot or to seek new solutions.

Hence, the medium-term outlook is good timing for both parties as it fits the organizational needs of both the corporate and startup, and it helps both teams revisit their "why" at the crucial juncture of the collaboration.

4.2.1 Coaching Strategies: Collective Purpose to Collective Goals

As alluded to earlier in the chapter, there is a need to translate vision into goals to achieve the vision. In a collaboration between two very distinct entities, the need for this work to be done is even more critical as both may share the same vision but take a different approach. Fundamentally, that is what makes startups unique and different from traditional corporate. A case in point would be that startups are encouraged to innovate in an existing market but to bring a unique solution with a high barrier of entry. By the nature of its being, a startup is motivated to take a path to vision that is uniquely different from a corporate.

The question now is how a coach could help both teams find the collective goals that are essential to the collaboration's success. Clutterbuck (2020) has suggested a simple but effective chain of descriptions to first define purpose and goals. This is to bring clarity to these two terms that have often confounded many. In the "chain," he also described how mission, strategy, and tactics play a crucial part in bringing a clear approach to translating purpose to goals.

The chain as described by Clutterbuck follows:

A. **Purpose:** The greater good we aim to achieve.
B. **Mission:** A subset of purpose, what we can achieve in bringing the good we have aimed to achieve. In other words, there could be multiple missions to achieve a purpose.
C. **Strategy:** How will we obtain and use the necessary resources to achieve the mission.
D. **Goals:** A set of time-bound objectives that could help us achieve the strategy set in place. SMART goals are one of the most popular frameworks for articulating and keeping track of goals set.
E. **Tactics:** Our response to events to keep track with goals set.

Clutterbuck (2020) has offered us a clear path to help startups and corporates navigate collaboration by setting clear goals that are built on a purpose, a collective purpose of their shared vision or the "ideal world" that they would like to build.

Next, let's examine each of these links that form the chain in the context of a startup corporate collaboration.

A Purpose

Although startups and corporates are often regarded as innovators, innovation is still an endeavor led by either the startup founder or the corporate's research and development team. It is still a fundamental human endeavor that underpins innovation and brings about new technology and solutions to the market. A successful collaboration that results in a minimum viable product is a human and team endeavor: the effort of a single human and collective humans.

Clutterbuck (2020) argues that success is about "achieving what you value," a truth that also applies to teams. He further added that "without a link to individual or collective values, which in turn link to purpose, short-term and medium-term achievements have little motivational effect."

So, to establish a collective purpose, which in higher performing teams involve a substantial blending of individual purpose with collective purpose (Clutterbuck, 2020), coaches need to help both startups and corporates in collaboration identify a shared or shared values.

Coaches can encourage all individuals to review their personal lives, especially during the developmental stages as teenagers, identify recurring themes, and note down where these themes continue to appear in their present selves. It is also critical to do some self-reflection about whether these recurring themes have shaped their decision-making and beliefs presently.

Once each team member of both parties can articulate their values, it is an opportune time to find a shared value as the core value upon which to build the shared purpose.

B Mission

At this stage, it will be a good opportunity to see how the technology brought in by the startup can contribute to the achievement of the mission. It is advisable to identify just one mission as to allow the innovation team to focus on while searching for a working collaborative model. This is also critical as it will allow the team to put its collective values into action.

If the team's values lead to eliminating illiteracy, then one mission could be to provide free education to the less fortunate.

The next question would be how the team sees that the technology or innovation they are collaborating on could help them achieve this mission. Their purpose-driven mission will guide their decision-making from design to delivery of a final minimum viable product.

Some of the questions that a coach could ask are:

- How could the technology or innovation we are working on achieve our purpose?
- How does the team know if the technology or innovation is helping us achieve our purpose?
- What checkpoints must we introduce to see if we are on route to achieving our mission?
- What would the final outcome look like?
- How would the team feel about the outcome?

C Strategy

Strategy is the "how" in achieving the mission. In the case of innovation, strategy is likely to center around the innovation or technology as it is the crux of the collaboration. This could be a potential pitfall to the collaboration's success, as the team may be tempted or unknowingly led by the technology's promises.

We have seen countless of such episodes when startup founders with promising technology abandoned their initial mission after being courted by investors such as venture capitalist. While it is not wrong to be courted or to court investors, startup founders must also understand that each investor, especially institutional investors such as venture capitalists, has a financial mandate the investor needs to fulfill. Hence, it is the venture capital prerogative to make suggestions for the startup's growth in a strategy that fits. However, that may be different from the startup's missions. Such startup founders will almost always be disillusioned; some may see they no longer have control over their startup. In the startup investment scene, it is much wiser to pursue what is known as "smart money," where the investor's and startup's strategies are aligned.

Therefore, the newly formed team must pay attention to not being led by technology but remaining faithful to the mission that was first identified. Only by doing so would the team not be forced to pivot the demand to the immediate need of their investors (likely to be corporate that sponsored the collaboration) or their clients (departments within the corporate looking to capitalize on the technology).

Another strong reason for the team to stay true to the mission is that only a team with high alignment of almost everyone to the mission that everyone is able to come behind the leader (Clutterbuck, 2020). This is especially important as, like any nascent project, the team must united in supporting the leader as the team is "feeling its way" to the next milestones. There will be pivoting: a term used commonly in the startup world, when a startup has to change the product's trajectory or refocus into a new market. All the above requires a strong and united team.

Some of the questions the coach could consider asking the team include the following:

- How does a strategy move the team closer to the mission?
- When is the right time to change strategy? What are some of the measurable items?
- What is informing the strategy? Is it the technology, the investor, the client, or the team?

D Goals

At the beginning of the chapter, we discussed the importance of SMART goals. As mentioned earlier, SMART goals possess certain qualities that can help a team achieve them, such as objectivity and time-bound measurement. They are simple and straightforward to understand.

However, Clutterbuck et al. (2013), in *Beyond Goals*, a coedited book, found that goal management is more complex than a simplistic approach allows. He and his fellow authors found that when "someone brings a goal to coaching, it represents their thinking so far" (Clutterbuck et al., 2013). This means that the goal can change in transformative coaching where the coachee is allowed the internal and external context that shapes the goal.

In other words, SMART goals can be determined only after a coaching conversation about what contributed to them. A deeper understanding of SMART goals can provide a much more effective goal-setting exercise, especially for a collaboration team with cultures that are poles apart.

The coach's role is to help the team return to the beginning of this chain during the goal-setting exercise. How is the goal related to the strategy, mission, and purpose?

Some of the questions the coach could ask are:

- Will the goal set help in executing the team's strategy?
- If it does not directly contribute to executing the strategy, will the goal advance the team's mission and purpose?

- Does the goal-setting exercise consider the technology or innovation central to the collaboration? If yes, will it hasten the achievement of the goal or hinder it?

E Tactics

Finally, we arrive at the end of the chain, which is tactics. Essentially, tactics are steps that we can take to achieve our goals, or in Clutterbuck's definition, our response to events to keep track of the goals set.

In the world of startups or even innovation, time is a luxury that startups do not have. The pace of advancement of technology, especially artificial intelligence, is astounding. Up until the year 2017, AI was a technology that had been around since World War II, but it didn't have the power to be generative.

The trajectory of the technology changed when a team of Google researchers led by Vaswani presented a seminal paper, titled "Attention Is All You Need" (Vaswani et al., 2017), with the introduction of the "transformer." To the uninitiated, the "transformer" is a new way of using what is known as the attention mechanism, which allows AI to weigh the importance of different words in a sentence. This allows the AI to "think" in a better context when forming sentences.

To further illustrate our point, ChatGPT, the generative AI tool by the company OpenAI, was first introduced in November 2022 and boasted 180 million users globally as of October 2024 (Duarte, 2024).

Therefore, there is a constant need to deploy or change tactics to keep up with such events in the startup world. The team will be constantly pressured to adopt and pivot the offering.

However, the team must remain faithful to the purpose, mission, strategy, and goals. In a coaching session, it is beneficial for the coach to create conversations based on the fundamentals that have already been agreed upon.

Some of the Questions the Coach Can Consider Asking

- In an ideal market where other technologies do not challenge the team's innovation, what are some of the tactics that can be deployed to move the team's purpose?
- Translating these tactics to the real world is fast changing; what else can be done?

Conclusion

A successful corporate–startup collaboration demands more than shared resources; it requires a shared vision that inspires both parties to pursue common objectives with purpose and passion. Chapter 4, "Shared Vision,

Shared Dreams," vividly demonstrates how a unified vision can bridge organizational divides and cultivate a sense of joint ownership, even in the face of different operating principles and pressures. When corporates and startups work together to create a vision that respects corporate legacy while embracing startup ingenuity, they unlock new levels of innovation and resilience, ushering in a new era of hope and potential for corporate–startup collaborations.

As illustrated throughout this chapter, the journey toward a shared vision requires active leadership, clear communication, and a commitment to translating purpose into actionable goals. As integral team members, coaches play a crucial role in this process, helping both parties remain aligned with their collective purpose and adapt strategies to meet evolving market demands. By establishing a shared vision, corporate and startup teams create a foundation of trust and a roadmap for collaborative growth, transforming shared dreams into tangible outcomes that benefit both the partnership and the broader market they serve.

Part III

The Collaborative Innovation

Chapter 5

Culture Is Key

Two major factors, related and dependent, are needed for corporate–startup collaboration and successful corporate innovation: culture and trust. This chapter delves into culture, and the next, "Trust Before Collaboration," will narrow down to trust.

Culture is one of the most decisive factors in corporate–startup collaborations, influencing every aspect of innovation, decision-making, and team dynamics. When corporates and startups join forces, their distinct cultural paradigms often clash. Corporates operate within structured hierarchies, emphasizing efficiency and risk management. In contrast, startups thrive on agility, creativity, and iterative experimentation. If left unaddressed, this cultural divide can lead to misalignment, misunderstandings, and failed partnerships.

Coaching plays a fundamental role in mitigating these cultural challenges, bridging differing values, working styles, and strategic objectives. Through coaching formulation, leaders and teams can systematically identify and address the root causes of cultural friction, fostering an environment where both entities can leverage their strengths. This chapter delves into the pivotal role of culture in corporate–startup collaborations, examining its impact on team dynamics, decision-making, and trust-building.

We explore real-world examples, including the Target–Chef'd collaboration, where cultural misalignment led to failure, and the case study of TechCorp and GreenMarket, which highlights how coaching strategies successfully navigated cultural differences. Additionally, we analyze the role of emotional intelligence (EI) in fostering cultural integration, emphasizing how self-awareness, adaptability, and relationship management can enhance collaboration. By prioritizing cultural alignment through targeted coaching interventions, organizations can unlock the full potential of their partnerships, ensuring sustainable innovation and long-term success.

Key Takeaways

- **Culture Defines Success:** The alignment of corporate and startup cultures is critical in determining the success or failure of open innovation collaborations.

DOI: 10.4324/9781003469155-8

- **Emotional Intelligence Is Essential:** Empathy, adaptability, and self-regulation are crucial in bridging cultural differences and improving team dynamics.
- **Misalignment Leads to Failure:** Real-world examples such as the Target–Chef'd project demonstrate how cultural misalignment can undermine even promising collaborations.
- **Coaching as a Bridge:** Strategic coaching interventions can facilitate cultural alignment, enhance communication, and build mutual trust between corporate and startup teams.
- **Hierarchical vs. Agile Cultures:** Large corporations typically operate with structured hierarchies, while startups emphasize flexibility and rapid decision-making, creating partnership frictions.
- **Trust Is a Byproduct of Culture:** Without cultural alignment, trust is difficult to establish, leading to increased risks of failed collaborations.
- **Systemic Coaching for Integration:** A systemic approach to coaching helps align team values, decision-making processes, and collaboration expectations.
- **Coaching Formulation for Problem-Solving:** Coaching formulation provides a structured framework for identifying and addressing the root causes of cultural misalignment in corporate–startup collaborations.
- **Case Study: TechCorp and GreenMarket:** The case study of TechCorp and GreenMarket highlights how coaching interventions help resolve cultural misalignment and drive effective collaboration.
- **Sustaining Cultural Synergy:** Ongoing coaching and reflective feedback loops are necessary to maintain alignment as corporate–startup relationships evolve.

5.1 The Rise and Fall of a Retail Corporate–Startup Collaboration

In 2015, a bold venture entered the burgeoning meal kit industry with ambitions to disrupt traditional food delivery. This company focuses on delivering high-quality, chef-curated meal kits without the constraints of a subscription model. The startup quickly gained attention in the market by offering fresh, preportioned ingredients and easy-to-follow recipes. It formed partnerships with renowned chefs and food brands, which appeared to secure its place in the industry. However, scaling the business and managing distribution presented significant challenges.

Meanwhile, a large retailer with a long history of innovation in the retail sector was keen to capitalize on the growing demand for convenient meal solutions. By 2018, this company sought to enhance its grocery segment by introducing new and innovative food options. Recognizing the potential of the meal kit industry, the retailer saw an opportunity to diversify its grocery offerings and gain market share in this fast-evolving sector.

The collaboration between the two companies was structured as a retail partnership. The startup began selling its meal kits in the retailer's stores across the United States, leveraging the extensive retail network to reach a broader audience. The meal kits are placed in the refrigerated sections of these stores to offer consumers fresh and convenient meal options. This partnership allowed the startup to move beyond its direct-to-consumer online model while the retailer diversified its grocery offerings.

However, despite the initial optimism, the partnership faced significant hurdles. The meal kits struggled to gain traction due to their high price points and the stiff competition from other providers offering similar options at lower prices. Sales failed to meet expectations, and within months of launching in the stores, the startup ceased operations, citing financial difficulties and an inability to scale effectively.

Cultural differences between the two companies further complicated the partnership. The retailer, as a large and established entity, prioritized efficiency, cost control, and broad market appeal. On the other hand, the startup operated with a more innovative and agile culture but needed help with the operational demands required to meet the retailer's needs. The differences in business models and priorities created friction. While the retailer emphasized affordability and convenience for its customers, the startup focused on premium pricing and quality, leading to a misalignment in market strategy.

This misalignment, coupled with the inability to scale and maintain competitive pricing, ultimately led to the collapse of the collaboration. After the startup's closure in July 2018, its assets were acquired by another company, which continued to sell meal kits under a different model. Meanwhile, the retailer shifted its focus to other meal kit providers, continuing its efforts to innovate within the grocery sector without relying on the premium pricing model.

The startup's founder, Kyle Ransford, reflected on the experience, saying, "We underestimated the complexities of scaling up to meet the demands of a large retail partnership" (Ransford, 2018, p. 63). A spokesperson from the retailer echoed the sentiment, acknowledging that while the concept of meal kits held promise, the collaboration taught valuable lessons about aligning with partners who share a commitment to affordability and accessibility (Target Corporation, 2018, p. 47).

The companies at the center of this collaboration were Chef'd and Target. Chef'd, founded in 2015 by Kyle Ransford, sought to disrupt the meal kit industry with its high-quality, chef-curated offerings. Target, a retail giant established in 1902 by George Dayton, aimed to diversify its grocery segment by partnering with Chef'd. Despite the potential, cultural differences and market challenges ultimately led to the partnership's collapse, with Chef'd ceasing operations just months after launching its products in Target stores.

5.2 A Clash of Cultures

A clash of cultures is highly likely in a corporate innovation scenario where a large corporation collaborates with startups, as seen in the Target–Chef'd collaboration in the previous section. The corporate environment and the startup ecosystem operate under different cultural norms, which can lead to friction if not managed effectively.

1   **Organizational Hierarchy vs. Flexibility:** Large corporations typically have established hierarchies, formal processes, and a risk-averse culture, which often aligns with Hofstede's dimensions of high power distance and uncertainty avoidance. On the other hand, startups thrive on flexibility, rapid decision-making, and innovation, often embodying a culture akin to Cameron and Quinn's adhocracy type, where creativity and agility are prized (Cameron & Quinn, 2011, p. 34).
2   **Speed of Execution:** Startups move quickly to capture market opportunities, driven by urgency. However, corporations may have slower decision-making processes due to their size and the need for consensus, which can frustrate startup partners accustomed to a more dynamic pace. This difference can lead to a clash, particularly in project timelines and expectations.
3   **Risk Appetite:** Startups typically have a higher tolerance for risk, viewing failure as a learning opportunity. In contrast, corporations may be more conservative, focusing on minimizing risk and protecting their existing business. This divergence in risk tolerance can create tension, especially when the corporate partner perceives innovative ideas from the startup as too risky (Deming, 2000, p. 89).
4   **Communication and Decision-Making Styles:** Corporations often have formal communication channels and decision-making processes, which startup teams can see as bureaucratic. Startups usually favor informal, direct communication and quick decision-making, which can lead to misunderstandings or perceived disrespect if not navigated carefully (Schein, 2016, p. 23).
5   **Cultural Integration Challenges:** Cultural differences can hinder the process when a corporate partner attempts to integrate a startup's innovation into its operations. Schein's concept of underlying assumptions is particularly relevant here; if the corporate culture's deep-seated beliefs about how things should be done are not aligned with the startup's approach, resistance can arise, making integration difficult (Schein, 2016, p. 30).

5.2.1 Addressing the Clash of Cultures

To mitigate the clash of cultures, both sides must consciously bridge the gap through the following:

Cultural Awareness and Sensitivity: Both the corporation and the startup must recognize and respect their cultural differences. Open communication about expectations, values, and working styles can help prevent misunderstandings (Hofstede, 2001, p. 78).

Adaptive Leadership: Leaders on both sides should adopt a flexible leadership style that can accommodate the cultural strengths of both the corporate and startup environments. This includes fostering an environment where the startup's innovation can thrive without being stifled by corporate bureaucracy (Kotter, 2012, p. 65).

Shared Vision and Goals: Establishing a shared vision and clear goals from the outset can help align both parties, reducing the potential for cultural clashes. This shared purpose can serve as a unifying force that transcends cultural differences (Cameron & Quinn, 2011, p. 56).

In conclusion, while a clash of cultures in open innovation collaborations between corporates and startups is almost inevitable, it does not have to be a roadblock. With intentional strategies and mutual respect, these cultural differences can be harnessed to drive innovation and create value for both parties.

> Our belief is that if you get the culture right, most of the other stuff—like great customer service, or building a great long-term brand, or passionate employees and customers—will happen naturally.
> —Tony Hsieh, former CEO of Zappos

Tony Hsieh, the visionary former CEO of Zappos, made corporate culture the cornerstone of his business philosophy. He believed that culture is the foundation of everything in a business. He famously stated that his goal was to create a company culture so strong that even if Zappos's business model became obsolete, the company would still thrive because of its people. Hsieh believed that culture is not just one aspect of the game; it is the game. He understood that a positive and engaging workplace would naturally lead to motivated employees and exceptional customer service. This customer-centric culture was a key factor in Zappos's success and growth, ultimately leading to Amazon's acquisition of $1.2 billion in 2009.

The success of Zappos under Hsieh's leadership is a testament to his belief that a strong, positive culture is the foundation of a successful business.

5.3 Culture Is Key

In corporate–startup collaborations within open innovation, culture is a critical determinant of success. It influences innovation, financial performance, and employee retention and impacts other vital business outcomes, such as customer satisfaction, brand reputation, and operational efficiency. These factors collectively contribute to the overall success and sustainability of the collaboration. The complexities of integrating distinct corporate and startup cultures demand deliberate and strategic management, as the stakes are higher than simply aligning internal teams; the collaboration must also resonate externally with stakeholders, customers, and the market.

The Multifaceted Influences of Culture

Impact on Innovation: Innovation, often seen as the most direct outcome of cultural alignment, flourishes in environments where creativity, collaboration, and agility are encouraged. When corporate and startup cultures align, they can harness their respective strengths—corporates provide resources and stability, while startups bring fresh perspectives and speed. This synergy leads to groundbreaking innovations that neither entity could achieve alone. As Schein (2010) highlighted, a strong culture fosters creativity and risk-taking, which are essential components of innovation (p. 28).

The collaboration between General Motors (GM) and Lyft, for example, demonstrated how cultural alignment could drive innovation. GM's resources and experience in the automotive industry, combined with Lyft's innovative approach to ride-sharing, resulted in the development of autonomous vehicle technology. The cultural alignment between the two companies, which emphasized shared goals and open communication, was crucial in enabling this innovation (Thompson, 2016).

Financial Performance: Financial outcomes are directly tied to the effectiveness of culture in collaborations. When cultures align, resources are used efficiently, and decision-making processes are streamlined, leading to cost savings and improved profitability. Misaligned cultures, however, can lead to wasted resources, delays, and financial losses. Weber and Camerer (2003) found that companies with aligned cultures experience higher financial returns, while those with cultural conflicts often see decreased profitability (p. 409). The collaboration between Amazon and Whole Foods illustrates how cultural alignment can drive financial success. Despite initial concerns about the culture clash between the tech giant and the organic food retailer, Amazon integrated its data-driven, customer-focused culture with Whole Foods's emphasis on quality and sustainability. This alignment has increased both companies' market share and profitability (Stone, 2017).

Employee Retention and Engagement: Employee retention and engagement are crucial for maintaining the momentum of a collaboration. Employees who feel aligned with the collaborative culture are more likely to stay committed and productive. Denison and Mishra (1995) emphasize that companies with strong, adaptable cultures see higher employee retention and engagement, which translates into sustained performance (p. 215). In corporate–startup collaborations, where cultural differences can create tension, creating a unified culture that resonates with employees from both entities is essential. This reduces turnover and fosters a sense of belonging, ultimately enhancing productivity and collaboration.

Customer Satisfaction: Culture also plays a significant role in customer satisfaction. When corporate and startup cultures align, they can deliver products and services that meet or exceed customer expectations. A shared culture that prioritizes customer-centricity ensures that both entities work toward providing value to customers, leading to higher satisfaction rates. Apple and its collaboration with various app developers demonstrate this principle. Apple's culture of design excellence and user experience aligns with developers who share these values, leading to high-quality apps that enhance customer satisfaction. This alignment has contributed to Apple's reputation as a leader in customer satisfaction (Isaacson, 2011).

Brand Reputation: A robust and aligned culture also impacts brand reputation. In a corporate–startup collaboration, the public perception of both entities can be influenced by how well they work together. A positive, aligned culture signals the market that the collaboration is strong and that the products or services they deliver are trustworthy and high quality. Nike's collaboration with the startup RTFKT in the NFT and digital apparel space is a prime example. Nike's brand, known for innovation and pushing boundaries, aligns with RTFKT's futuristic vision. This cultural alignment has enhanced Nike's reputation as a forward-thinking company, resonating well with the younger, tech-savvy demographic (Hughes, 2021).

Operational Efficiency: Operational efficiency is another bottom line affected by culture. When cultures are aligned, processes are more streamlined, and collaboration becomes more efficient. This reduces the time-to-market for new products and services, minimizes operational costs, and improves overall productivity. The partnership between Toyota and Tesla showcases how cultural alignment can drive operational efficiency. Toyota's lean manufacturing principles and Tesla's innovative approach to electric vehicles created a synergy that enhanced operational processes for both companies during their collaboration (Liker, 2004).

Complexity of Corporate–Startup Collaboration Culture: Managing the culture in corporate–startup collaborations is inherently more complex than managing a single company's culture. Structured hierarchies, formalized processes, and risk aversion often characterize corporations. Startups, on the other hand, operate with agility, informality, and a higher tolerance for risk. Bridging these cultural differences requires more than just alignment—it demands a strategic approach to integration. Nahapiet and Ghoshal (1998) argue that building social capital, which includes shared norms, trust, and networks, is crucial for managing the complexities of collaboration culture (p. 245). In this context, collaboration culture must not only align with the strategic objectives of both entities but also adapt to the unique demands of the partnership. This creates a more dynamic and flexible culture, which differs significantly from the relatively stable culture within a single organization.

Culture serves as the cornerstone of success in corporate–startup collaborations within open innovation. It impacts various business outcomes, including innovation, financial performance, employee retention, customer satisfaction, brand reputation, and operational efficiency. Compared to a single company's culture, the complexity of managing a collaboration culture requires deliberate efforts to align values, practices, and communication styles. When managed effectively, cultural alignment not only drives successful collaborations but also enhances the bottom line for both corporate and startup partners.

5.4 Navigating Team Dynamics: The Role of Emotional Intelligence in Shaping Collaborative Culture

Understanding the culture within corporate–startup collaborations necessitates an in-depth examination of team dynamics, with emotional intelligence (EI) at its core. Culture in these partnerships is not an abstract concept but a tangible force shaped by the individuals' interactions, behaviors, and emotional competencies (Goleman, 1995, p. 43). The success or failure of collaboration often hinges on how well the teams from different organizational backgrounds align in their goals and processes. Here, team dynamics play a pivotal role. Misalignments in communication styles, decision-making approaches, and conflict-resolution methods can derail even the most promising ventures (Tannenbaum et al., 1992, p. 327). Emotional intelligence becomes the bridge that harmonizes these dynamics, enabling individuals to navigate conflicts, build trust, and foster a collaborative spirit (Cherniss, 2001, p. 93). As we explore further, the intricate relationship between team dynamics and EI will reveal how these elements jointly cultivate a sustainable and transformative culture in corporate–startup collaborations.

5.4.1 Why Emotional Intelligence?

Emotional intelligence (EI) is indispensable in the team dynamics of open innovation teams due to the unique and multifaceted challenges these teams face. Open innovation projects involve diverse groups of individuals—often from different organizations, industries, and cultural backgrounds—working together toward a common goal. This diversity brings a wealth of perspectives and ideas but also introduces the potential for conflict, miscommunication, and friction. EI is the cornerstone that enables team members to navigate these complexities effectively.

Firstly, collaboration within open innovation teams hinges on the ability of team members to empathize with one another. Empathy, a key component of EI, allows individuals to understand and appreciate their team members' perspectives, emotions, and motivations. This understanding is crucial when integrating ideas from different disciplines or industries, as it helps bridge the gaps between varying points of view and fosters a collaborative spirit (Goleman, 2004, p. 88). Without EI, team members may struggle to connect on a human level, leading to misinterpretations and a lack of cohesion.

Secondly, conflict resolution in open innovation teams demands high levels of EI. Conflicts are inevitable when individuals with diverse backgrounds and expertise come together. However, how these conflicts are managed can determine the success or failure of a project. EI equips team members with the skills to handle disagreements constructively. By recognizing and managing their emotions, individuals can engage in difficult conversations without escalating tensions, finding solutions that satisfy all parties involved. This ability to de-escalate potential conflicts and maintain harmony is essential for keeping the team focused on innovation rather than internal disputes (Bradberry & Greaves, 2009, p. 54).

Lastly, effective stakeholder management in open innovation projects requires keen EI. Stakeholders in such projects can range from internal team members to external partners, investors, and customers. Each group comes with its expectations, concerns, and emotional drivers. Leaders and team members with high EI can tailor their communication and engagement strategies to address these varying needs, building trust and ensuring all stakeholders feel valued and heard. This trust is critical for securing the long-term commitment and cooperation necessary for the success of open innovation initiatives (Boyatzis & McKee, 2005, p. 32).

In sum, EI is crucial in the dynamics of open innovation teams because it facilitates effective collaboration, enables constructive conflict resolution, and ensures successful stakeholder management. These elements are foundational to the success of any open innovation project, as they help harness the full potential of diverse teams working toward a shared vision.

5.4.2 Team Dynamics in Corporate–Startup Collaboration

Understanding the intricacies of team dynamics requires delving into the emotional intelligence (EI) of the individuals and the collective group involved in the collaboration. In the case of Chef'd and Target, discussed at the start of this chapter, the cultural differences that led to the downfall of their partnership also shed light on how critical aspects of EI—such as self-awareness, empathy, and relationship management—play a pivotal role in navigating these dynamics. Subsequent analysis will explore the behaviors and traits related to EI within the teams, examining how their interactions, communication styles, and decision-making processes influenced the outcome of the collaboration. This evaluation will reveal the crucial role that emotional intelligence plays in aligning team dynamics and ensuring the success of corporate partnerships.

5.4.3 Team Dynamics: Behaviors and Traits Relating to Emotional Intelligence

The case of Chef'd and Target Corporation reveals critical insights into how emotional intelligence (EI) directly affects team dynamics, especially in corporate partnerships. The failure of this collaboration was due not just to strategic misalignment but rather deep-seated issues rooted in the lack of EI across both organizations. By analyzing the dynamics at play, we can understand how both teams' emotional intelligence, or lack thereof, impacted the outcome.

Empathy Deficit in Team Interactions: Empathy is crucial in any collaboration, as it fosters understanding and cooperation between team members. In the Chef'd and Target partnership, empathy was notably absent. Target's team, focused on mass-market efficiency, failed to appreciate the challenges Chef'd faced in maintaining a high-quality product at scale. Conversely, Chef'd's team struggled to empathize with Target's cost-conscious retail environment (Wilson, 2018, p. 42). This lack of empathy created a disconnect between the two teams, preventing them from forming a cohesive strategy aligning with both companies' goals. When team members do not take the time to understand each other's perspectives, collaboration becomes superficial, leading to unresolved conflicts and, ultimately, failure.

Resistance to Adaptability: Adaptability, a core component of emotional intelligence, is particularly crucial in dynamic environments where flexibility is key to meeting evolving challenges. Both teams in the Chef'd and Target partnership exhibited resistance to adapt. Chef'd's team, while innovative, found it challenging to adjust their business model to fit the scale and distribution demands of Target's retail environment. This rigidity created friction, as Target's team expected more agility and responsiveness from their partner (Ransford, 2018, p. 63). On the other hand, Target's team was slow to adapt their expectations and support systems to accommodate Chef'd's premium product offering. In team dynamics, the inability to adapt often leads to stagnation and frustration, as members become entrenched in their positions rather than working together to find solutions.

Emotional Self-Regulation Challenges: Effective team dynamics rely on emotional self-regulation, which enables team members to manage stress, conflicts, and setbacks constructively. In this partnership, emotional self-regulation was lacking. As the challenges of scaling and distribution mounted, both teams struggled to maintain composure and focus. Chef'd's team, under pressure from unmet sales targets and operational difficulties, became increasingly reactive rather than proactive (Peters, 2018, p. 50). Target's team, in turn, grew frustrated with the lack of progress, leading to strained communications and a breakdown in trust. This inability to regulate emotions within the teams exacerbated existing tensions and hindered effective problem-solving.

Deficient Social Skills in Conflict Resolution: Social skills, particularly in communication and conflict resolution, are critical for maintaining positive team dynamics. In the case of Chef'd and Target, poor social skills on both sides contributed to the partnership's collapse. The teams struggled with clear communication, particularly around aligning their objectives and expectations (Wilson, 2018, p. 42). As conflicts arose—over pricing, product placement, or customer reception—neither team demonstrated the social acumen to navigate these challenges effectively. Research supports that strong social skills are essential for resolving conflicts and fostering collaboration within teams

(Bridoux & Stoelhorst, 2016, p. 210). This partnership's lack of these skills resulted in unresolved disputes and a gradual erosion of trust.

Lack of Emotional Awareness: Emotional awareness, the ability to recognize and understand one's emotions and those of others, plays a critical role in team dynamics. The Chef'd and Target teams did not have this awareness, leading to misunderstandings and misaligned priorities. For instance, Chef'd's team underestimated the emotional impact of their premium pricing strategy on Target's cost-conscious customer base. At the same time, Target's team did not fully grasp the emotional commitment Chef'd had toward maintaining quality, leading to frustrations on both sides (Ransford, 2018, p. 60). When team members lack emotional awareness, they are unable to anticipate and respond to each other's needs, leading to a breakdown in collaboration.

5.5 Case Study (Composite): Coaching for Effective Collaboration Between TechCorp and GreenMarket

5.5.1 Background and Coaching Strategy

Corporate–startup collaborations create opportunities for market expansion, innovation, and operational efficiency. However, these partnerships often face obstacles due to misaligned cultures, decision-making processes, and structural differences. This case examines the collaboration between TechCorp, a global e-commerce and logistics leader, and GreenMarket, a high-growth startup in organic grocery retail. The partnership sought to merge TechCorp's technological expertise with GreenMarket's market knowledge, but significant conflicts emerged.

Using the coaching formulation approach proposed by Lane, Corrie, and Kovacs (2025), this case identifies the underlying causes of these challenges. It explores how coaching interventions can align leadership, improve team engagement, and create strategic cohesion. The formulation process revealed that a fundamental clash of cultures lay at the core of the conflicts, requiring a structured and adaptive coaching response.

Why Coaching Formulation?

Coaching formulation was chosen over directive problem-solving or standard leadership development approaches because it allows for a systemic understanding of organizational conflicts. Unlike prescriptive models that impose solutions, coaching formulation facilitates collaborative sense-making, ensuring that leaders and teams coconstruct a path forward (Lane et al., 2025, p. 9). Formulation integrates multiple perspectives, including individual leadership behavior, team interactions, and systemic factors, which are critical in corporate-startup collaborations (Corrie & Kovacs, 2019, p. 14). This method also provides an iterative framework, allowing adjustments based on emerging insights and stakeholder input (Drake, 2011, p. 125).

Strategic Objectives

The collaboration sought to achieve the following goals:

1   **Operational Efficiency:** Optimize GreenMarket's supply chain by integrating TechCorp's logistics expertise.
2   **Technology Adoption:** Leverage automation and data-driven decision-making.
3   **Market Growth**: Use TechCorp's e-commerce platforms to expand GreenMarket's customer base.
4   **Cultural Alignment:** Balance TechCorp's efficiency-driven structure with GreenMarket's community-focused approach.

Coaching Formulation Findings: The Cultural Clash

Through the formulation process, coaching interventions revealed that cultural misalignment—not operational inefficiencies—was the root cause of resistance and dysfunction. TechCorp's standardized, data-centric decision-making clashed with GreenMarket's decentralized, values-driven culture. Employees at GreenMarket resisted new performance metrics imposed by TechCorp, perceiving them as undermining their autonomy. Longstanding suppliers struggled with the centralized procurement model, fearing the partnership would erode the trust-based relationships they had cultivated over the years (Lane et al., 2025, p. 14).

5.5.2 Coaching Interventions

The coaching interventions implemented the following solutions:

1   **Executive Coaching:** Leadership Alignment
    Leadership misalignment was a central issue. TechCorp's executives focused on scale and efficiency, while GreenMarket's leadership emphasized sustainability and community engagement. Coaching sessions helped both leadership teams articulate their priorities and cocreate a shared vision. Executive coaching facilitated reflective exercises, encouraging TechCorp's leaders to recognize the strategic value of GreenMarket's relational approach and helping GreenMarket's executives adapt to performance-driven structures (Flaherty, 2010, p. 78).
2   **Team Coaching:** Employee Adaptation
    TechCorp's structured processes disrupted GreenMarket's flexible work culture. Employees expressed concerns about losing their identity within a corporate system prioritizing automation over relationships. Team coaching applied collaborative inquiry methods, enabling employees to voice their concerns and contribute to the adaptation process. By contextualizing new performance metrics within GreenMarket's mission,

coaching sessions helped employees see alignment between efficiency and sustainability (Clutterbuck et al., 2016, p. 39).

3   **Systemic Coaching:** Supplier Integration

Suppliers viewed TechCorp's procurement model as transactional, contrasting GreenMarket's relational sourcing strategy. Coaching supported negotiations between GreenMarket and TechCorp's procurement teams, ensuring that supplier relationships were preserved while optimizing costs. Systemic coaching provided a structured framework for balancing efficiency with long-term partnerships (O'Neill, 2007, p. 102).

A Coaching Conversation Example

Scenario: Addressing the cultural misalignment in the TechCorp–Green-Market collaboration.

Context: This team coaching conversation occurs between a team coach and a mixed group of TechCorp and GreenMarket employees struggling with cultural misalignment following their companies' collaboration. The goal is to facilitate alignment through team coaching, using the coaching formulation approach to surface key concerns and create a shared understanding (Lane et al., 2025, p. 9). Team coaching is instrumental in fostering collective problem-solving and enhancing team cohesion by addressing underlying tensions (Clutterbuck et al., 2016, p. 39).

COACH: Thank you all for being here today. I understand that the collaboration between TechCorp and GreenMarket has created some challenges, particularly around culture and work expectations. My role is to help us explore these challenges and find a way forward together. To start, can someone share an experience where you felt the differences between the two organizations most strongly?

GreenMarket Employee 1: Honestly, I feel like we've lost our sense of autonomy. At GreenMarket, we used to have the freedom to make decisions based on what was best for our customers and suppliers. Now, everything is dictated by centralized processes from TechCorp.

TechCorp Employee 1: From our side, I see that structure and standardization help us scale effectively. But I hear your frustration. Maybe we need to discuss where flexibility can still exist within these processes?

COACH: That's a great insight. The tension between autonomy and standardization is common in collaborations like this. What impact do you think this tension is having on your ability to work together?

GreenMarket Employee 2: It's creating a lack of trust. Our suppliers feel pushed out because they don't fit into TechCorp's procurement model.

And internally, we feel like we don't have a voice in decision-making anymore.COACH: Trust is key to any successful partnership (Clutterbuck et al., 2016, p. 41). Let's explore that further. What specific actions could help rebuild trust between teams and with suppliers?

TechCorp Employee 2: Maybe we need more open discussions, like this, where both sides feel heard. We could also create a hybrid approach—keeping some flexibility in procurement while applying TechCorp's efficiencies where they add real value.

COACH: That's an excellent starting point. The coaching formulation approach encourages a cocreated solution rather than a one-sided decision (Corrie & Kovacs, 2019, p. 14). What commitments can we make today to ensure these ideas turn into action?

GreenMarket Employee 1: We can set up regular feedback sessions with suppliers so they feel included.
TechCorp Employee 1: And we can create a task force with team members from both companies to review where flexibility can be maintained without disrupting efficiency.

COACH: Those sound like actionable steps. Let's document these commitments and set a check-in date. I'll also be available to facilitate ongoing coaching discussions as needed. Sustained team coaching ensures long-term behavioral change, so ongoing dialogue will be essential (Clutterbuck et al., 2016, p. 45). Thank you all for your engagement today.

5.5.3 Outcomes and Reflection

Breakthrough and Progress

The collaboration between TechCorp and GreenMarket transformed significantly through targeted coaching interventions. Initially, cultural friction obstructed progress, as GreenMarket employees resisted TechCorp's structured, efficiency-driven approach, while TechCorp executives struggled to integrate GreenMarket's relationship-centric business model. The coaching formulation process illuminated these cultural gaps and provided a structured path toward resolution (Lane et al., 2025, p. 14).

Executive coaching enabled leadership teams to develop a shared vision that blended TechCorp's operational rigor with GreenMarket's customer-centric ethos (Flaherty, 2010, p. 78). Leaders from both organizations cocreated a governance framework that allowed GreenMarket to maintain autonomy in areas critical to its identity while adopting TechCorp's logistical efficiencies, where they added measurable value.

Team coaching sessions helped employees from both organizations better understand their respective work cultures. By reframing TechCorp's data-driven approach as a tool to support—rather than replace—GreenMarket's human-centric decision-making, coaching facilitated greater buy-in (Clutterbuck et al., 2016, p. 39). Employees who initially resisted new performance metrics became active participants in shaping their implementation, ensuring alignment with GreenMarket's values.

Systemic coaching addressed tensions with GreenMarket's long-standing suppliers, who feared losing personalized relationships in TechCorp's centralized procurement model. Through guided negotiations, TechCorp adapted its processes to preserve supplier relationships while introducing scalable efficiencies (O'Neill, 2007, p. 102). The result was a hybrid procurement strategy that upheld trust-based partnerships while achieving cost optimizations.

By the end of the engagement, the partnership had moved beyond surface-level compromises to a deeply integrated collaboration that leveraged the strengths of both organizations. TechCorp gained access to new markets through GreenMarket's brand loyalty, while GreenMarket scaled efficiently without sacrificing its core values. The case underscored that cultural integration, not just operational alignment, determines the success of corporate–startup collaborations (Corrie & Kovacs, 2019, p. 14).

Coach's Reflection

This case reinforced that if left unaddressed, cultural misalignment can derail even the most strategically sound partnerships. TechCorp and GreenMarket's challenges were not due to flawed business logic but to fundamentally different organizational philosophies. The coaching formulation approach proved essential in uncovering these underlying tensions and enabling both sides to collaboratively design solutions rather than imposing unilateral fixes (Lane et al., 2025, p. 9).

One of the most significant insights was the power of executive coaching in shifting leadership mindsets. TechCorp's leadership initially viewed GreenMarket's flexible approach as inefficient, while GreenMarket's executives feared TechCorp's standardization would erode their identity. Coaching helped both sides recognize that efficiency and relationship-driven business models were not mutually exclusive (Drake, 2011, p. 125). By reframing differences as complementary strengths, leaders moved from opposition to collaboration.

The impact of team coaching was equally profound. Employees from both companies initially approached the integration with skepticism, seeing it as a forced adaptation rather than an opportunity. Coaching facilitated open conversations where employees expressed concerns without fear of retaliation. Once they felt heard, they became instrumental in shaping a hybrid culture that honored both companies' strengths (Clutterbuck et al., 2016, p. 45).

Systemic coaching played a crucial role in supplier negotiations. GreenMarket's suppliers, accustomed to personal relationships, perceived TechCorp's approach as purely transactional. Coaching created a bridge, helping TechCorp appreciate the strategic value of trust-based sourcing while guiding GreenMarket's suppliers through a structured transition (Corrie & Kovacs, 2019, p. 14).

Ultimately, the success of this coaching intervention highlighted that culture is not an obstacle to overcome but an asset to leverage. Corporate–startup collaborations thrive when coaching enables leaders and teams to navigate differences, embrace new perspectives, and build shared frameworks that balance efficiency with human connection. Future partnerships should approach cultural alignment as a strategic imperative, integrating coaching from the outset to mitigate conflicts before they escalate.

Conclusion

The TechCorp–GreenMarket collaboration underscores the importance of cultural alignment in corporate–startup partnerships. Coaching formulation identified cultural friction as the primary challenge and provided a structured framework to address leadership misalignment, employee resistance, and supplier concerns. The partnership moved toward a more cohesive and sustainable collaboration by employing executive, team, and systemic coaching interventions. Future corporate–startup partnerships must recognize the central role of cultural integration and leverage coaching formulation to navigate complexities effectively.

Discussion Questions

1   How does coaching formulation enhance problem-solving in corporate–startup collaborations?
2   What coaching techniques can strengthen leadership alignment in cross-organizational partnerships?
3   How can systemic coaching preserve stakeholder relationships in a corporate-driven operational shift?
4   What role does coaching play in maintaining startup agility while integrating with a corporate structure?

Conclusion

Culture is the linchpin of corporate–startup collaborations, influencing everything from innovation capacity to operational effectiveness. This chapter has explored how cultural misalignment can derail partnerships, using real-world examples such as the Target–Chef'd collaboration and the in-depth case study of TechCorp and GreenMarket. These cases illustrate that while cultural differences are inevitable, they do not have to be insurmountable barriers. The right coaching strategies can transform these challenges into opportunities for stronger, more resilient collaborations.

Coaching plays a fundamental role in bridging cultural gaps. Through coaching formulation, organizations can systematically diagnose and address the underlying tensions that arise from cultural differences. Rather than applying one-size-fits-all solutions, coaching formulation encourages collaborative sense-making, ensuring that all stakeholders contribute to defining a shared path forward. This approach is particularly valuable in corporate–startup collaborations, where differences in hierarchy, speed, and risk appetite can create tension.

The TechCorp–GreenMarket case study exemplifies the power of targeted coaching interventions in navigating cultural misalignment. Leadership coaching helped executives align their strategic vision, team coaching facilitated communication and adaptability among employees, and systemic coaching ensured that stakeholder relationships remained intact. These interventions collectively enabled the partnership to overcome its cultural challenges and move toward a sustainable, high-performing collaboration.

Trust, a critical factor in any collaboration, emerges naturally when cultural alignment is established. As coaching helps integrate different working styles, decision-making processes, and expectations, it fosters an environment where trust can grow. This, in turn, enables teams to work more cohesively, driving both innovation and operational efficiency.

Ultimately, organizations that recognize culture as a key determinant of success in corporate innovation will be better positioned to thrive in today's dynamic business landscape. Investing in coaching strategies that emphasize cultural alignment, emotional intelligence, and trust-building will not only mitigate risks but also unlock the full potential of corporate–startup collaborations. As the next chapter explores, trust is the next critical pillar that must be cultivated for successful and enduring collaborations.

References

Coaching Formulation and Strategic Coaching Approaches

Corrie, S., & Kovacs, L. C. (2019). *Coaching and complexity: Understanding clients through formulation*. London: Routledge.

Drake, D. B. (2011). *Narrative coaching: The definitive guide to bringing new stories to life*. San Francisco, CA: CNC Press.

Lane, D. A., Corrie, S., & Kovacs, L. C. (2025). *A guide to formulation in coaching*. London: Routledge.

Team Coaching and Cultural Alignment

Clutterbuck, D., Megginson, D., & Bajer, A. (2016). *Building and sustaining a coaching culture: A developmental approach*. London: CIPD Publishing.

Hawkins, P. (2021). *Leadership team coaching in practice: Case studies on developing high-performing teams*. London: Kogan Page.

O'Neill, M. B. (2007). *Executive coaching with backbone and heart: A systems approach to engaging leaders with their challenges.* San Francisco, CA: Jossey-Bass.
Corporate-Startup Collaboration & Organizational Culture
Chesbrough, H. (2020). *Open innovation results: Going beyond the hype and getting down to business.* Oxford: Oxford University Press.
Edmondson, A. C. (2019). *The fearless organization: Creating psychological safety in the workplace for learning*, innovation, and growth. Hoboken, NJ: Wiley.
Schein, E. H., & Schein, P. A. (2017). *Organizational culture and leadership* (5th ed.). Hoboken, NJ: Wiley.

Chapter 6

Trust Before Collaboration

In corporate innovation, trust is not just an abstract value but a prerequisite for success. Without trust, even the most well-funded, strategically aligned partnerships crumble under the weight of miscommunication, misalignment, and competing priorities. In fast-moving environments where corporations and startups collaborate, trust becomes even more critical as both entities operate with distinct cultures, risk appetites, and decision-making processes.

Coaching serves as a crucial bridge to cultivate trust between corporate and startup teams. Effective coaching strategies guide leaders through the complexities of trust-building by addressing emotional intelligence, cultural adaptation, and transparent communication. By equipping leaders with the skills to foster trust, coaches play a pivotal role in transforming fragmented, misaligned teams into cohesive, high-functioning collaborators.

This chapter explores coaching strategies that help corporate and startup leaders navigate trust challenges, from systemic coaching interventions to structured communication frameworks. It examines the role of emotional intelligence in trust-building, the impact of leadership behaviors on team dynamics, and the practical application of coaching models like the GROW framework and David Clutterbuck's team coaching approach. Through real-world case studies, this chapter highlights how trust—or the lack of it—determines the outcome of corporate–startup partnerships.

By integrating coaching into trust-building efforts, organizations can mitigate the risks associated with collaboration and unlock the full potential of their partnerships. Coaches facilitate this transformation by fostering environments where trust is not just a passive expectation but an actively cultivated foundation for innovation and long-term success.

Key Takeaways

- **Trust Must Be Intentionally Cultivated:** Trust does not develop by default in corporate–startup collaborations. Coaches implement structured interventions, such as trust-building exercises, leadership alignment

DOI: 10.4324/9781003469155-9

coaching, and conflict resolution frameworks, to ensure trust is embedded in the partnership from the outset.

- **Emotional Intelligence Is the Foundation of Trust:** Leaders must develop self-awareness, empathy, and emotional regulation to foster trust. Coaches facilitate this through targeted emotional intelligence coaching, including reflective exercises, active listening training, and self-regulation practices that enhance leadership effectiveness in collaborative environments.
- **Cultural Integration Requires Coaching Support:** Corporations and start-ups operate with different mindsets. Corporations prioritize stability and compliance, while startups thrive on agility and risk-taking. Coaches use systemic coaching techniques to help leaders navigate these cultural differences, aligning values and operational expectations to reduce friction and establish a shared vision.
- **Leadership Coaching Strengthens Trust-Building Behaviors:** Trust in teams stems from leadership behaviors. Coaches work with corporate and startup leaders to model trust-building behaviors like transparency, vulnerability, and accountability. Through executive coaching sessions, leaders develop the skills to set clear expectations, communicate openly, and handle conflicts constructively.
- **Structured Communication Protocols Prevent Trust Erosion:** Trust breaks down when communication lacks clarity and consistency. Coaches introduce structured communication frameworks, such as regular check-ins, transparent reporting, and feedback loops, to create an open flow of information. These protocols prevent misunderstandings and reinforce trust between teams.
- **Systemic Coaching Aligns Leadership Teams:** Misalignment between corporate and startup leadership can fracture trust. Coaches use systemic coaching to diagnose leadership misalignment, address power dynamics, and establish collective accountability. This intervention ensures that both entities operate from a position of mutual respect and shared strategic intent.
- **Trust-Building Exercises Reinforce Psychological Safety:** Teams cannot innovate without psychological safety, which is built on trust. Coaches design trust-building workshops that include role-reversal exercises, conflict mediation training, and scenario-based problem-solving sessions. These exercises create an environment where team members feel safe sharing ideas and collaborating effectively.
- **A Structured Road Map for Trust-Building:** Formulation in coaching serves as the diagnostic foundation, using the *4P framework* (*Purpose, Perspective, Process, and Positionality*) to identify trust deficits. Once assessed, targeted coaching models—*GROW, CLEAR*, and *team coaching*—guide leadership development and trust restoration. This integration ensures a structured yet adaptable approach, making trust-building efforts precise, strategic, and sustainable in corporate–startup collaborations.

- **Continuous Coaching Ensures Long-Term Trust Stability:** Trust-building is not a one-time event; it requires ongoing reinforcement. Coaches implement long-term coaching programs, including quarterly trust audits, leadership recalibration sessions, and strategic collaboration reviews, to maintain trust even as partnerships evolve.
- **Coaching Transforms Trust Into a Competitive Advantage:** Organizations that embed coaching into their trust-building efforts gain a strategic edge. By ensuring trust remains a core pillar of their collaboration culture, companies unlock sustained innovation, resilience, and long-term success in corporate–startup collaborations.

6.1 The Challenges: The Issue on Trust

6.1.1 The Grab–OYO Collaboration: Lessons in Trust and Business Alignment

The partnership between Southeast Asia's ride-hailing behemoth, Grab, and India's disruptive budget hotel chain, OYO, was a much-anticipated collaboration. With both companies sharing the ambition of market dominance, their strategic alliance appeared to be a win-win for both parties. This case offers insight into how high-stakes collaborations can falter when trust and operational alignment fail to keep pace with market ambitions.

Collaboration Context

Grab's journey into becoming a super-app was driven by the desire to integrate various services into one platform, capturing multiple facets of users' daily lives. Partnering with OYO allowed Grab to expand its offerings into the travel and hospitality sector, allowing users to book hotels directly through the app. On the other hand, OYO had been aggressively expanding its footprint beyond India and saw Grab as a pivotal partner to tap into the Southeast Asian market.

Anthony Tan, CEO of Grab, and Ritesh Agarwal, founder and CEO of OYO, were the key figures driving this partnership. Both leaders aimed to leverage their companies' unique strengths to create a combined force that could outmaneuver local competitors. Agarwal, known for his bold expansion strategies, envisioned OYO's rapid growth across Southeast Asia. Tan, determined to diversify Grab's offerings, believed this collaboration would further cement Grab's status as the leading super-app in the region (Tan, 2021, p. 56).

Collaboration Structure

The strategic partnership involved Grab investing in OYO while integrating OYO's services into the Grab app. The goal was twofold: to boost Grab's super-app strategy and offer OYO an immediate customer base in Southeast Asia. This collaboration also aligned with Grab's broader expansion into nontransport services, following its ventures into food delivery and financial services. OYO's value lies in budget accommodations in key markets such as Singapore, Thailand, and Indonesia.

At first, the partnership appeared seamless. Both companies hailed the deal as a breakthrough in creating a comprehensive user experience. As part of their vision, Tan remarked, "The future of super-apps lies in connecting every aspect of our customers' lives" (Tan, 2021, p. 57). Agarwal echoed this sentiment: "OYO's reach, combined with Grab's platform, would revolutionize how people travel across Southeast Asia" (Agarwal, 2021, p. 104).

Trust Issues and Operational Misalignment

However, beneath the surface, tensions began to arise. OYO's aggressive expansion, which involved acquiring many properties and rapidly scaling operations, raised concerns within Grab. OYO had been facing scrutiny for its fast-growth tactics, which critics argued compromised the quality of its services. Additionally, OYO's controversial approach to contract renegotiations with hotel owners created reputational risks for Grab. A Grab executive shared, "The operational inconsistencies and rising complaints about OYO's services were becoming too much to ignore" (Chin, 2021, p. 92).

Trust between the companies began to erode, especially when Grab's internal evaluations revealed a growing misalignment with OYO's practices. OYO's penchant for making headline-grabbing expansion moves appeared at odds with Grab's more measured approach to sustainable growth. This dissonance led Grab to reassess the future of the collaboration.

By mid-2020, as OYO's expansion in Southeast Asia began to stall, Grab gradually distanced itself from the partnership. Trust issues stemming from concerns over OYO's operations and business practices ultimately led to the fading of this once-promising partnership. As Tan later remarked, "We had to prioritise long-term trust over short-term market gains" (Tan, 2021, p. 58).

Outcome

The collaboration, once touted as a powerful alliance, fizzled out quietly. Grab reduced its involvement with OYO, choosing to refocus its energy on core services such as food delivery and digital finance. On the other hand, OYO shifted its focus back to stabilizing its operations and rebuilding trust with hotel partners, stepping away from its hypergrowth strategy. Ultimately, the partnership served as a cautionary tale of how misaligned business practices and trust issues can undermine even the most promising collaborations.

This case highlights the fragility of partnerships, especially in fast-evolving markets where trust, operational transparency, and alignment are paramount. Both Grab and OYO walked away with valuable lessons on the importance of long-term sustainability over short-term expansionism.

6.2 The Complexities in Corporate Startup Collaboration

Corporate–startup collaboration culture is a complex and multifaceted phenomenon that requires navigating distinct organizational paradigms. Corporations, with their entrenched hierarchies and rigid processes, often exhibit a cautious approach to risk. In contrast, startups thrive on agility, informality, and a propensity for embracing uncertainty. This divergence necessitates a cultural alignment and a thoughtful integration strategy to harmonize these disparate approaches.

As described by Nahapiet and Ghoshal (1998), the concept of social capital emphasizes the importance of shared norms, trust, and networks in managing collaboration culture (p. 245). Social capital builds the foundation for mutual understanding and trust, which is essential in bridging the gap between corporate rigidity and startup fluidity. This dynamic becomes particularly relevant in collaborations where both entities must constantly adapt to each other's evolving needs and market conditions. In this context, collaboration culture diverges from the relatively stable culture found within a single organization and requires a more dynamic and flexible approach.

The importance of cultural integration in corporate–startup collaborations extends beyond mere social capital. It requires both parties to establish a shared vision and understand their partnership goals. According to Schein (2010), successful cultural integration hinges on the ability of both entities to engage in "cultural dialogue," where differences are openly discussed and mutual respect is fostered (p. 325). This cultural dialogue becomes a cornerstone for building a collaborative environment that leverages the strengths of both parties.

Furthermore, research by Chesbrough (2003) on open innovation underscores the necessity of cultural adaptability. Corporations must embrace a more open and decentralized approach to innovation, while startups must learn to navigate the corporate landscape without losing their entrepreneurial spirit (p. 57). The interplay between corporate structure and startup agility requires a nuanced understanding of maintaining innovation without succumbing to bureaucratic inertia.

In practice, building a collaborative culture involves continuous effort in aligning both strategic objectives and daily operations. Kale, Singh, and Perlmutter (2000) highlight the importance of alliance learning processes, where both parties actively learn from each other to overcome cultural barriers and enhance their collaboration (p. 221). This iterative process of learning and adaptation fosters a culture that is both resilient and innovative, capable of responding to the challenges inherent in corporate–startup collaborations.

Moreover, the role of leadership in managing collaboration culture cannot be understated. Leaders from both entities must champion the integration process, modeling the behaviors and values that they wish to see within the partnership. As Gino and Staats (2015) argue, leaders play a pivotal role in setting the tone for collaboration by fostering a culture of experimentation and continuous improvement (p. 8). This leadership-driven approach helps mitigate the potential cultural clash and ensures that the partnership remains focused on shared success.

Finally, the collaboration culture in corporate–startup partnerships must remain adaptable. As Puranam, Alexy, and Reitzig (2014) suggest, a culture that embraces ambiguity and is willing to evolve over time will better navigate the inevitable challenges of collaboration (p. 829). This adaptability enables the partnership to remain aligned with both internal and external changes, ensuring long-term success.

Managing the culture of corporate–startup collaborations involves a strategic integration of social capital, cultural dialogue, alliance learning, and leadership. By embracing these elements, corporations and startups can create a dynamic and flexible culture that leverages their respective strengths and adapts to the unique demands of their partnership.

6.3 Trust: A Pillar in Positive Team Dynamics

Understanding the complexities in corporate–startup collaboration demands a closer examination of the dynamics within the teams involved. While vital, cultural integration between corporations and startups does not exist in isolation. Trust becomes a critical pillar that not only underpins this integration but also ensures the long-term success of the collaboration. Trust is necessary for even the most well-structured cultural strategies to succeed. The intricacies of team dynamics, particularly in a collaboration where diverse organizational cultures converge, require trust as their foundation. This trust, cultivated through emotional intelligence (EI) and reinforced by clear and consistent communication, enables both entities to navigate the inherent uncertainties of their partnership. As Mayer, Davis, and Schoorman (1995) assert, trust fosters psychological safety, empowering team members to contribute meaningfully and engage fully (p. 713). This engagement is crucial in corporate–startup collaborations, where agility and stability are needed to drive innovation.

Furthermore, the role of leadership in cultivating trust cannot be overstated. Leaders who model emotionally intelligent behavior set the tone for trust within the partnership, creating an environment where collaboration can thrive. Therefore, to truly grasp the complexities of corporate–startup collaboration, one must analyze team dynamics, and trust is pivotal to bridging the cultural divide.

In cultivating positive dynamics within a working team, trust, EI, and communication are interdependent elements that shape the team's success. Understanding their interrelation offers an understanding for building effective teams that perform well and exhibit resilience in the face of challenges.

6.4 Emotional Intelligence as a Catalyst for Trust

Emotional intelligence plays a crucial role in developing and sustaining trust within a team. When team members display high emotional intelligence—through self-awareness, empathy, and effective regulation of emotions—they become more predictable and reliable in their interactions. This consistency fosters trust, as others perceive them as emotionally stable and considerate (Goleman, 1998, p. 43). For example, a leader who remains calm under pressure and listens empathetically during conflicts reinforces the trust that others have in them. Thus, emotional intelligence acts as a catalyst, accelerating the development of trust by ensuring emotionally intelligent behaviors that inspire confidence.

6.5 Communication as the Reinforcement of Trust

Communication is not just a means of conveying information but a powerful tool that solidifies trust within a team. Transparent, consistent, and emotionally intelligent communication ensures that team members remain aligned, reducing misunderstandings and reinforcing trust (Lencioni, 2002, p. 28). Trustworthy communication involves not only the words spoken but also the nonverbal cues and active listening that convey respect and understanding. In teams where communication flows openly and without fear of judgment, trust deepens, enabling more robust collaboration and innovation. A team that communicates with both clarity and empathy strengthens its trust foundation, making it more resilient in the face of challenges.

6.6 The Synergy in Trust, Emotional Intelligence, and Communication

The synergy between trust, emotional intelligence, and communication creates a positive feedback loop that enhances team dynamics. Trust allows emotional intelligence to flourish by providing a safe emotional expression and understanding space. In turn, emotional intelligence promotes behaviors reinforcing trust, such as empathy and self-regulation. Communication then acts as the mechanism that ties these elements together, ensuring that trust and emotional intelligence are consistently practiced and reinforced within the team (Druskat & Wolff, 2001, p. 132). For instance, a study found that high-trust teams, characterized by open communication and emotional awareness, achieved higher performance levels (Salovey & Mayer, 1990, p. 190).

In conclusion, trust is a vital component of positive team dynamics, enabling the development of emotional intelligence and effective communication. By cultivating trust, teams create an environment where members feel safe to express themselves, collaborate openly, and innovate without fear of failure. Emotional intelligence sustains this trust by promoting empathy and emotional stability, while communication reinforces it through clear and empathetic exchanges. Leaders and coaches who prioritize trust will find that it creates a ripple effect, enhancing team dynamics and performance.

6.6.1 Successful Business Leaders Value Trust

Successful business leaders like Jack Ma view trust as a significant foundation of their leadership philosophy and organizational success. For Jack Ma, trust is not merely a leadership trait but a strategic imperative that empowers teams to perform at their best. His belief that "trust is the most important thing in business" underscores its role in building solid and high-functioning teams. Ma consistently embedded trust into Alibaba's culture, viewing it as the foundation for innovation, problem-solving, and collaboration.

Jack Ma on Trust

> Trust is the most important thing in business. I believe in my team. I trust them because they are trustworthy.
>
> —Jack Ma, Cofounder of Alibaba

Jack Ma, cofounder of Alibaba, built one of the world's largest e-commerce platforms by deeply embedding trust into the company's culture. Ma consistently emphasized that trust within his team was fundamental to Alibaba's growth and success. This principle of trust was not just a leadership philosophy; it was the foundation of how Alibaba operated internally and externally. Ma believed that a trustworthy team was the key to innovation, problem-solving, and overcoming challenges (Ma, 2016, p. 37).

At the core of Ma's leadership style was his unwavering trust in his team. He understood that empowering his team members through trust would unleash their full potential, fostering a culture of loyalty, collaboration, and shared responsibility. This approach was evident in several critical areas of Alibaba's development:

1   **Empowerment Through Trust:** Ma believed that the best leaders trusted their teams to make decisions and take ownership of their work. At Alibaba, he delegated authority to his team, allowing them to innovate and take risks. This trust empowered employees to contribute ideas, take initiative, and push boundaries. Ma's trust in his team was reflected in his hands-off approach to management, where he provided guidance but allowed his team the freedom to execute strategies independently. This approach created a strong sense of ownership among Alibaba's employees, driving the company's success (Fan, 2017, p. 140).

2   **Collaboration and Innovation:** Trust was also the cornerstone of collaboration at Alibaba. Ma encouraged open communication and teamwork, believing that a culture of trust would lead to better collaboration and, ultimately, more significant innovation. For instance, Alibaba's rapid expansion into cloud computing and digital payments was driven by cross-departmental collaboration, where team members trusted one

another's expertise and worked together to create new solutions. This trust-based teamwork was crucial to Alibaba's ability to innovate and stay ahead in the competitive tech industry (Clark, 2016, p. 65).

3   **Resilience in Adversity:** Ma's trust in his team became particularly evident during difficult times. When Alibaba faced setbacks, such as the challenges during the dot-com bubble burst and the global financial crisis, Ma's trust in his team helped the company navigate uncertainty. He relied on his team's commitment and expertise, trusting that they would find ways to adapt and overcome challenges. This mutual trust created a strong sense of solidarity, which was essential for Alibaba's resilience and eventual recovery (Wu, 2020, p. 196).

4   **Building a Loyal Workforce:** Trust also played a critical role in building loyalty within Alibaba's workforce. Ma believed that when leaders trusted their employees, it fostered a reciprocal trust that led to long-term loyalty. This loyalty was a significant factor in Alibaba's ability to retain talent and maintain a cohesive team, even as the company proliferated. Employees who felt trusted by Ma and the leadership team were more likely to stay committed to Alibaba's mission and vision, contributing to the company's sustained growth (Ma, 2016, p. 44).

5   **Legacy of Trust:** Jack Ma's emphasis on trust within his team has left an enduring legacy at Alibaba. His belief that trust was the foundation of teamwork drove Alibaba's internal success and shaped the company's reputation externally. The culture of trust that Ma cultivated continues to influence Alibaba's operations, ensuring that the company remains innovative, resilient, and a trusted partner in the global business community (Fan, 2017, p. 144).

6.7 Case Study: Coaching Strategies for Trust-Building in a Corporate-Startup Collaboration

This composite case study illustrates the deliberate choice of coaching strategies deployed and the coaching model that structured the coaching intervention.

Corporate–startup collaborations often succeed or fail based on factors beyond strategy or resources. Trust and EI play a pivotal role in shaping the outcomes of these partnerships. While corporate giants bring stability and infrastructure, startups contribute agility and innovation, sparking exciting possibilities. However, when leadership styles clash, cultural differences emerge, or communication breaks down, even the most promising ventures can quickly unravel. Trust, more than just a foundation, is a critical enabler for progress. When trust erodes, relationships strain, and innovation stalls. The case of Stellar Pharmaceuticals and BioTech Innovators underscores this reality. Conflicting priorities and leadership friction threatened to derail a collaboration designed to revolutionize personalized medicine. Through this case, we explore how coaching interventions can address these issues, rebuild trust, and realign leadership to create a path forward.

6.7.1 Case Study (Composite): The Stellar Pharmaceuticals and BioTech Innovators Collaboration

Stellar Pharmaceuticals, a global pharmaceutical leader, and BioTech Innovators, a biotech startup, launched a collaboration to advance personalized medicine. Strategic misalignments, leadership friction, and cultural differences quickly strained the partnership. This case study examines how coaching interventions, structured through Formulation in Coaching by Lane, Corrie, and Kovacs (2025, p. 72), reestablished trust, enhanced emotional intelligence, and aligned leadership dynamics.

Learning Outcomes

By the end of this case study, readers will be able to:

1   Understand how the Formulation in Coaching model applies to corporate–startup collaborations.
2   Identify the role of trust-building and emotional intelligence in leadership alignment.
3   Analyze systemic and behavioral factors that contribute to partnership challenges.
4   Evaluate different coaching models for conflict resolution and strategic alignment.
5   Develop strategies to integrate structured coaching frameworks in innovation-driven environments.

The Case

Stellar Pharmaceuticals, known for its expertise in chronic disease treatments, sought to expand into personalized medicine through gene therapy. It partnered with BioTech Innovators, a young company specializing in CRISPR-based gene editing. The collaboration was structured as a corporate innovation initiative, with Stellar handling clinical trials and regulatory processes while BioTech provided the gene-editing technology. However, fundamental differences quickly eroded trust.

Origins of the Trust Breakdown

Mistrust between the companies emerged from conflicting priorities. Stellar Pharmaceuticals emphasized regulatory compliance and patient safety, while BioTech Innovators prioritized speed and market positioning. Dr. Murray, Stellar's chief scientific officer, adhered to a methodical, risk-averse approach, ensuring adherence to stringent regulatory protocols. In contrast, BioTech's CEO, Dr. Reid, championed rapid experimentation and industry disruption.

Their divergent leadership styles led to friction, stalled decision-making and frequent clashes in strategic direction.

Tensions escalated when BioTech Innovators independently accelerated prototype development without Stellar's full approval. The move triggered concerns about oversight and control, reinforcing Stellar's fears about regulatory risks. BioTech viewed Stellar's reluctance as bureaucratic inertia, further straining the relationship. The absence of a structured mechanism for conflict resolution compounded the issue, highlighting the need for targeted coaching interventions.

About the Coach

The coach, a seasoned professional with over 15 years of experience in leadership development and corporate innovation, has a strong track record of guiding organizations through complex challenges in collaboration and innovation. As a member of the European Mentoring and Coaching Council (EMCC), the coach adheres to the highest ethical standards and practices in coaching, ensuring a structured, results-oriented approach to their work.

With a background in coaching both large multinational corporations and emerging startups, the coach specializes in navigating the unique challenges of corporate–startup collaboration. Their expertise lies in helping teams overcome obstacles such as leadership misalignment, cultural friction, and communication breakdowns, which often plague such collaborations. This experience has given the coach a deep understanding of the nuanced dynamics between corporate structures and agile startups, particularly the need to bridge the gap between different leadership styles, cultural priorities, and strategic objectives.

In addition to direct coaching, the coach has mentored numerous startup founders, helping them navigate the challenges of scaling their businesses, securing partnerships, and aligning their vision with long-term goals. By focusing on emotional intelligence, trust-building, and transparent communication, the coach empowers teams to foster collaboration and drive innovation, even in high-stakes environments.

Their coaching approach is informed by evidence-based methodologies and real-world experience, allowing them to tailor strategies that promote sustainable change. Committed to continuous learning and professional development, the coach regularly engages in advanced training and contributes to discussions on best practices in corporate innovation coaching, making them a thought leader in the field.

The Role of the Coach

The coach acted as an intermediary, ensuring both leaders recognized their blind spots and adjusted their behaviors. The coach facilitated open dialogues through structured interventions, helping both parties appreciate each other's constraints and strengths. The coach established a foundation for trust restoration and long-term collaboration by emphasizing active listening and empathy exercises.

6.7.2 Formulation in Coaching Approach

The Role of Formulation in Coaching

The Formulation in Coaching model provides a structured assessment of coaching needs by diagnosing interpersonal dynamics, systemic influences, and cognitive patterns that hinder collaboration. It emphasizes a 4P framework—*purpose, perspective, process*, and *positionality*—to structure interventions effectively (Lane et al., 2025, p. 74). This method moves beyond predefined coaching techniques by crafting tailored solutions based on a deep understanding of client behavior and team interactions.

Assessing the Coaching Context

- **Cognitive and Emotional Influences**: Dr. Murray (Stellar Pharmaceuticals) prioritized patient safety and regulatory compliance, while Dr. Reid (Bio-Tech Innovators) focused on speed and market impact. Their divergent mindsets fueled resistance and misalignment (Goleman, 1998, p. 114).
- **Behavioral and Systemic Factors**: Stellar Pharmaceuticals operated within a structured hierarchy, while BioTech Innovators thrived on agility. These conflicting cultures exacerbated communication breakdowns (Clutterbuck, 2013, p. 53).

Coaching Contract and Initial Interventions

The coaching contract formalized expectations, emphasizing transparency and accountability. The initial phase focused on increasing self-awareness, challenging assumptions, and aligning expectations (Covey, 2004b, p. 219). Real-time behavioral analysis and feedback loops structured the process to track progress.

Discussion Questions

1   How does the Formulation in Coaching model enhance the effectiveness of coaching interventions?
2   What are the key differences in leadership approaches between Dr. Murray and Dr. Reid?
3   How does the 4P framework contribute to diagnosing interpersonal and systemic challenges?
4   What role does transparency play in establishing an effective coaching contract?

6.7.3 Coaching Interventions

Collaborative Trust-Building Exercises

Using Cognitive Behavioral Coaching (Neenan & Palmer, 2001, p. 64), the intervention targeted the following deep-seated assumptions and reactive behaviors:

- **Challenging Assumptions**: Leaders engaged in structured dialogues to surface and challenge unconscious biases.
- **Empathy Development**: Role-reversal exercises forced each leader to experience the constraints of the other's responsibilities.
- **Psychological Safety Protocols**: Facilitated discussions and established norms for candid, constructive exchanges (Edmondson, 2018, p. 97).

Emotional Intelligence (EI) Enhancement

Lane, Corrie, and Kovacs (2025, p. 126) emphasize EI as a fundamental driver of leadership effectiveness. The coaching intervention focused on:

- **Self-Regulation Training**: Mindfulness exercises reduce reactive decision-making.
- **Active Listening**: Leaders engaged in structured listening exercises to eliminate defensive communication patterns (Boyatzis, 2008, p. 146).
- **Emotional Data Reflection**: Leaders maintained journals to track emotional responses and their impact on decision-making (Goleman, 1998, p. 137).

Leadership Realignment Through Multiple Coaching Models

- CLEAR Coaching Model (Hawkins, 2012, p. 84): Structured conversations to define Challenges, Listen actively, Explore options, Agree on actions, and Review progress.
- GROW Model (Whitmore, 2017, p. 45): Leaders defined Goals, assessed Reality, explored Options, and determined the Way forward.
- Transformational Coaching (Bass, 1990, p. 99): Focused on shifting leadership behaviors to drive collective change.

Discussion Questions

1   How do role-reversal exercises contribute to building empathy in leadership?
2   What impact does psychological safety have on conflict resolution in team dynamics?
3   How can self-regulation training improve decision-making in high-pressure situations?

4   What are the benefits of integrating multiple coaching models in leadership realignment?

6.7.4 Outcomes and Reflection

Breakthrough and Resolution

Months into the coaching process, leaders redefined their strategic outlook. Dr. Murray acknowledged the importance of agility, while Dr. Reid recognized the necessity of regulatory adherence. Coaching interventions produced the following tangible outcomes:

- A structured strategic road map balancing innovation speed with compliance.
- Leadership teams are committed to transparent communication and mutual respect.
- A sustainable framework for ongoing trust-building and conflict resolution.

Measuring Coaching Impact

To demonstrate the effectiveness of coaching, the following measurable indicators were established:

- Decision-Making Efficiency: Reduced approval timelines for joint initiatives by 30%.
- Collaboration Metrics: Increased alignment in strategic planning sessions, leading to a 40% decrease in unresolved conflicts.
- Employee Sentiment: Internal surveys reflected a 25% increase in confidence in the partnership's sustainability.

Coaching sessions employed cognitive behavioral coaching techniques to reshape assumptions and introduce practical solutions (Neenan & Palmer, 2001, p. 64). Role-reversal exercises required Dr. Murray and Dr. Reid to experience the challenges of each other's domains, deepening their understanding and empathy (Edmondson, 2018, p. 97).

Ensuring Long-Term Collaboration

Restoring trust requires more than immediate conflict resolution. To maintain alignment, structured governance mechanisms were introduced:

- Trust Audits: Quarterly assessments ensured ongoing transparency in decision-making.

- Joint Leadership Workshops: Regular sessions reinforced collaboration strategies and emotional intelligence practices.
- Governance Frameworks: A structured review board facilitated open discussions, preventing strategic drift.

The companies ensured that past tensions would not resurface by embedding trust-building measures within operational frameworks. As a result, both leaders shifted their perspectives—Dr. Murray acknowledged the value of agility, while Dr. Reid embraced regulatory adherence as a critical component of long-term success.

Coach's Reflection

Applying multiple coaching models provided a comprehensive solution to trust erosion. The intervention restored collaboration by integrating cognitive, emotional, and systemic dimensions. Trust, emotional intelligence, and cognitive realignment emerged as critical elements in sustaining corporate–startup partnerships (Lane et al., 2025, p. 126).

Discussion Questions

1 What were the primary factors that led to the initial trust breakdown?
2 What key factors contributed to the resolution of trust issues between the leaders?
3 How does a structured coaching road map help maintain a balance between innovation and compliance?
4 How did coaching interventions reshape leadership behaviors?
5 How can structured governance mechanisms ensure long-term collaboration?
6 What lessons can future corporate–startup collaborations draw from this case study?

Case Conclusion

This case study highlights the essential role of structured coaching in restoring trust and alignment in corporate–startup collaborations. Trust does not develop automatically—it must be built through consistent actions, transparent communication, and leadership alignment. The breakdown between Stellar Pharmaceuticals and BioTech Innovators stemmed from deeply rooted differences in priorities, leadership styles, and operational structures. Coaching interventions helped bridge these divides, introducing clear frameworks that transformed conflict into constructive dialogue.

The coaching strategy focused on emotional intelligence, role clarity, and structured decision-making. Using targeted coaching models such as the 4P framework, cognitive behavioral coaching, and transformational coaching, both organizations gained a structured method to resolve disputes and reestablish confidence in the collaboration. These interventions ensured that the leaders did not merely manage their differences but learned to leverage them for more significant innovation.

Sustaining this trust required more than behavioral shifts. The introduction of governance mechanisms—trust audits, structured leadership workshops, and review boards—cemented a long-term commitment to transparency and accountability. This approach reinforced trust as an ongoing process rather than a one-time repair.

Ultimately, this case study proves that coaching is not just a remedial tool but a strategic asset in corporate innovation. Organizations that embed coaching into their collaboration strategies can preempt conflicts, align leadership, and create environments where innovation thrives. The lessons from this partnership serve as a blueprint for any company seeking to navigate the complexities of corporate–startup relationships while maintaining trust and strategic alignment.

Conclusion

Trust forms the foundation of every successful corporate–startup partnership. Without it, even the most well-planned collaborations become susceptible to misalignment, strategic drift, and eventual failure. This chapter has demonstrated that trust is not an incidental byproduct of collaboration but a deliberate outcome that requires structured coaching interventions.

Corporate innovation demands more than shared objectives; it requires leaders who understand and embody trust-building behaviors. Coaching plays a crucial role in equipping these leaders with the skills necessary to cultivate trust through emotional intelligence, transparent communication, and structured interventions. Emotional intelligence serves as a key driver of trust, as leaders with heightened self-awareness and empathy can navigate conflicts more effectively and build stronger relationships within teams. By guiding leaders through the development of emotional intelligence, coaches help foster an environment where trust becomes a cultural norm rather than an exception.

The Grab and OYO example and Stellar Pharmaceuticals and BioTech Innovators case study illustrate how trust deficits can derail partnerships despite strong strategic intent. The Grab–OYO collaboration initially seemed like a perfect alignment of ambitions, but operational misalignment and growing distrust ultimately led to its dissolution. Similarly, Stellar Pharmaceuticals and BioTech Innovators struggled with leadership friction, conflicting priorities, and cultural misalignment, jeopardizing their shared vision for advancing personalized medicine. These examples reinforce a fundamental truth—trust is not self-sustaining. It requires continuous reinforcement through structured governance, clear expectations, and proactive conflict resolution.

Coaches play a vital role in designing and implementing trust-building exercises tailored to corporate–startup collaborations. By incorporating models such as the GROW framework and systemic coaching, they help leaders establish a shared vision, define transparent processes, and address misalignment before it escalates into conflict. Trust-building exercises, such as role-reversal dialogues and psychological safety protocols, further strengthen relationships by ensuring that corporate and startup leaders understand each other's constraints and motivations.

Another key takeaway from this chapter is that trust is not solely a leadership issue—it is embedded within an organization's culture. A lack of trust manifests in rigid hierarchies, siloed communication, and defensive decision-making. To counteract these tendencies, coaches introduce structured communication protocols such as regular check-ins, open forums, and structured feedback loops that reinforce transparency and accountability. These protocols ensure that trust remains an ongoing priority rather than a one-time initiative.

Sustaining trust in corporate innovation requires more than a short-term intervention. Trust audits, leadership workshops, and governance mechanisms provide long-term safeguards that maintain alignment even as market conditions evolve. Successful collaborations recognize that trust must be nurtured over time, with continuous coaching as the linchpin reinforcing trust across leadership teams and organizational structures.

Ultimately, trust is both an enabler and a competitive advantage. Companies prioritizing trust in their corporate–startup collaborations unlock higher levels of innovation, agility, and long-term resilience. Conversely, organizations that neglect trust risk undermining even their most strategic partnerships. By embedding coaching into trust-building efforts, leaders ensure that trust is not left to chance but intentionally cultivated as a core pillar of innovation.

Coaches act as the architects of trust, designing interventions that strengthen relationships, mitigate conflict, and create environments where collaboration thrives. Their role is indispensable in helping corporate and startup leaders navigate the complexities of trust-building, ensuring that innovation partnerships achieve their full potential. Trust is not merely a prerequisite for collaboration—it is the defining factor determining whether collaborations succeed or fail in the long run.

References

For further reading on coaching strategies, trust-building, and emotional intelligence, the following sources are recommended:

Edmondson, A. C. (2018). *The fearless organization: Creating psychological safety in the workplace for learning, innovation, and growth.* Wiley.

Goleman, D. (1998). *Working with emotional intelligence.* Bantam Books.

Hawkins, P. (2012). *Creating a coaching culture: Developing a coaching strategy for your organization*. McGraw-Hill.

Lane, D. A., Corrie, S., & Kovacs, L. (2025). *A guide to formulation in coaching*: Routledge.

Neenan, M., & Palmer, S. (2001). Cognitive behavioural coaching. *The Psychologist, 14*(2), 63–66.

Whitmore, J. (2017). *Coaching for performance: The principles and practice of coaching and leadership*. Nicholas Brealey Publishing.

Part IV

The Ecosystem of Innovation

Chapter 7

Progressive Pivoting

In today's volatile business environment, the ability to pivot determines whether organizations adapt or become obsolete. Pivoting is not merely a response to failure; it is a proactive strategy to remain competitive. In corporate–startup collaborations, progressive pivoting is especially crucial, allowing teams to realign strategies, explore new opportunities, and sustain long-term growth. Unlike a singular, drastic shift, progressive pivoting is a continuous process shaped by market shifts, customer feedback, and technological advancements.

This chapter examines the role of leadership, team engagement, and coaching strategies in enabling successful pivots. It explores real-world cases such as Airbus and Layer's collaboration, illustrating how strategic pivots demand strong team alignment, emotional intelligence, and systemic coaching interventions. The analysis underscores that pivots fail not due to flawed strategies but because of disengaged teams, misalignment, and resistance to change.

Additionally, Section 7.4 provides a detailed case study on the NexusTech–MindZen collaboration, demonstrating how coaching interventions turned a struggling corporate–startup partnership into a successful strategic pivot. The case study highlights the application of coaching methodologies, including the GROW model, systemic coaching, Formulation in Coaching, and psychological safety, which played a critical role in realigning the partnership. It underscores that coaching is not just a support mechanism but a vital element in navigating uncertainty and ensuring sustained engagement.

Effective coaching provides the necessary framework to navigate these challenges. By fostering team cohesion, facilitating courageous conversations, and reinforcing a shared vision, coaches empower teams to embrace pivots as opportunities rather than disruptions. This chapter offers theoretical insights and practical strategies to equip coaches, corporate leaders, and innovators with the tools to guide their teams through successful pivots.

DOI: 10.4324/9781003469155-11

Key Takeaways

- **Pivoting as an Ongoing Process:** Corporate innovation requires continuous adaptation, particularly within open innovation frameworks. Coaching helps teams stay agile and responsive to market changes.
- **Strategic Coaching for Effective Pivots:** Targeted coaching interventions ensure smoother transitions by addressing team dynamics, resistance, and alignment challenges. Applying systemic coaching, team coaching, leadership coaching, and Formulation in Coaching provides the necessary support to navigate these complexities.
- **Team Engagement as the Foundation of Pivots:** Sustained engagement through open communication, shared ownership, and clear objectives enhances the success of strategic shifts. Coaching methodologies such as appreciative inquiry, psychological safety, and Formulation in Coaching reinforce engagement.
- **Shared Vision Between Corporate and Startup Entities:** A unified vision strengthens collaboration, ensuring both parties align their strategic objectives during pivots. Systemic coaching frameworks help facilitate this alignment by addressing organizational interdependencies.
- **Emotional Intelligence in Change Management:** Leaders with high emotional intelligence navigate pivots more effectively, balancing corporate and startup teams' contrasting cultures and work styles. Coaching for emotional intelligence development enhances leadership adaptability.
- **Courageous Conversations Drive Alignment:** Honest, structured discussions resolve conflicts, clarify goals, and keep teams focused during periods of uncertainty. The GROW model and Formulation in Coaching provide structured approaches to facilitating these conversations.
- **Appreciative Inquiry as a Tool for Successful Pivots:** Leveraging strengths rather than solely focusing on deficiencies enhances team morale and supports smooth transitions. Coaches use appreciative inquiry to build on what works and encourage innovation.
- **Systemic Coaching for Sustained Alignment:** Addressing structural, strategic, and cultural differences through systemic coaching minimizes friction and enhances collaboration. Coaches employ systems thinking and Formulation in Coaching to effectively align multiple stakeholders.
- **Team Coaching to Strengthen Collaboration:** Focused coaching enhances team cohesion and enables the effective execution of pivots. Clutterbuck's team coaching framework provides tools for fostering shared leadership and accountability.
- **Continuous Learning for Adaptation:** Teams that cultivate a learning mindset remain adaptable to technological shifts and evolving market demands. Coaching strategies such as reflective learning and experiential coaching facilitate continuous learning.

- **Sustainability-Driven Pivots:** Incorporating sustainability into pivot strategies meets broader market expectations while enhancing long-term competitiveness. Coaching helps leaders integrate sustainability-driven goals into their strategic pivots.
- **Sustaining Innovation Through Pivots:** A culture of continuous innovation, adaptability, and open communication is essential for long-term corporate success. Coaching frameworks such as the GROW model, Formulation in Coaching, and systemic coaching ensure organizations maintain momentum in innovation.

7.1 The Challenges in Pivoting

The corporate–startup collaborations between Careem and Didi Chuxing in the Middle East and North Africa (MENA) region, and Rocket Internet with Lazada in Southeast Asia, provide insightful examples of ambitious strategic collaborations that ultimately faltered. Both cases showcase how startups aimed to pivot and leverage the strengths of global partners to strengthen their market positioning. Yet, despite strong external partnerships and sound strategic planning, neither collaboration succeeded.

The strategic collaboration between Careem, a Dubai-based ride-hailing startup, and Didi Chuxing, China's leading ride-hailing platform, commenced in 2018, with the intention of enhancing Careem's operations through the integration of artificial intelligence (AI) and data analytics. The partnership aimed to improve driver efficiency and optimize ride pricing by leveraging Didi's advanced technological capabilities. However, despite initial optimism, the collaboration failed, primarily due to a significant lack of workforce engagement within Careem.

Careem's employees, accustomed to a highly localized and customer-focused service model, struggled to adapt to the demands of Didi's data-driven technology. The transition required employees to shift from a service model grounded in regional expertise to one based on algorithms and AI-powered decision-making. This shift proved challenging, as Careem failed to provide the necessary training and communication to align its workforce with the new strategic objectives. Taneja et al. (2019) emphasize that "pivoting to AI-based solutions requires not only technological adoption but also a re-alignment of human resources, which was notably absent in the Careem-Didi collaboration" (p. 77). This misalignment caused operational inefficiencies and compounded the difficulties already present, as Didi struggled to navigate the complexities of the MENA market (Sarhan & Ahmed, 2020, p. 203). Consequently, Careem's teams remained disconnected from the collaboration's objectives, and the goals of the partnership remained unmet. The failure to engage employees in the strategic pivot, coupled with Didi's inability to localize its approach effectively, ultimately led to the dissolution of the collaboration. In 2019, Uber acquired Careem, marking the end of this ill-fated partnership (Natarajan, 2020, p. 213).

Similarly, Rocket Internet's pivot with Lazada highlights the pivotal role of workforce engagement in ensuring the success of strategic transformations. Lazada, launched by Rocket Internet in 2012, had rapidly become one of Southeast Asia's leading e-commerce platforms. However, in response to growing competition from major global players such as Alibaba and Amazon, Rocket Internet attempted to transform Lazada from a consumer-focused marketplace into a logistics and data-centric platform. This strategic shift aimed to strengthen Lazada's supply chain operations, yet failed due to a lack of internal engagement and communication with the company's workforce.

Lazada's employees, previously focused on customer acquisition and marketing, found themselves ill-prepared for the pivot toward complex logistics operations. Kerr et al. (2014) argue that the pivot represented "a fundamental change in business operations, but Lazada's workforce was not adequately prepared or trained for the shift" (p. 36). This lack of preparation resulted in widespread internal resistance, leading to declining morale and increasing staff turnover (Christensen et al., 2016, p. 87). Furthermore, Rocket Internet's top-down management approach obstructed effective communication between Lazada's leadership and its teams, exacerbating the operational challenges (Westerman et al., 2014, p. 44).

As Lazada struggled to align its workforce with the new strategic objectives, operational failures increased in frequency, leading to growing customer dissatisfaction. In 2016, Rocket Internet sold its controlling stake in Lazada to Alibaba, marking the failure of the strategic pivot and Lazada's subsequent reliance on external acquisition for its survival (Schaal, 2017, p. 49). This case further illustrates how inadequate workforce engagement during periods of strategic transformation can derail promising initiatives, particularly in rapidly evolving markets.

Both the Careem–Didi and Rocket–Lazada cases underscore the critical importance of employee engagement in driving successful pivots. In both instances, a lack of effective communication, insufficient training, and misalignment between management and employees led to operational failures, ultimately culminating in the dissolution of the collaborations. These examples demonstrate that technological advancements and external partnerships alone cannot guarantee the success of strategic shifts; internal alignment and team engagement remain essential for achieving desired outcomes.

7.2 Why Pivot?

Understanding the difficulties of pivoting, why is it imminent that businesses must pivot? Pivoting is an indispensable concept in the entrepreneurial process and growth, particularly for startups and corporates facing challenging market conditions. The strategic maneuver of pivoting allows businesses to change and modify their models or offerings in response to feedback, competition, or changing market needs.

7.2.1 Pivoting Is a Necessity and Continuous Process

The search results emphasize that the ability to pivot has become essential for organizations to survive and thrive in rapidly changing environments. Business leaders assert that pivoting is not merely a strategic option but a critical necessity, especially in light of technological disruptions and shifting consumer behaviors (Humans of Globe, n.d., p. 1).

Pivoting is not a one-time event but rather an ongoing process. For example, the article on famous startups that pivoted notes that "Matching the products offered to the real needs of consumers is beneficial for the development of any type of business," implying that pivoting should be a continuous effort to align with evolving customer demands (Humans of Globe, n.d., p. 2).

The research study on entrepreneurial pivoting in tech startups also found that "the value proposition can be created and sustained through pivoting." This suggests that pivoting is not just about making a single strategic shift but rather a means to continuously create and maintain a strong value proposition (Sala et al., 2022, p. 1051).

Next are the definitions and insights derived from various academic sources and business literature.

7.2.2 Definitions of Pivoting

In Startups

Strategic Redirection: Pivoting in startups is defined as a strategic shift in the business model or product offering, often initiated after recognizing that the current approach is not yielding the desired results. This is an essential shift for startups to realign their value proposition with market demands (Flechas et al., 2021, p. 888).

Feedback-Driven Adaptation: Startups often pivot based on feedback from customers or market conditions. This process involves testing new hypotheses about the business model and making necessary adjustments to enhance product-market fit (Burnell et al., 2023, p. 7).

Lean Startup Methodology: The lean startup framework emphasizes pivoting as a response to validated learning. Entrepreneurs are encouraged to experiment, gather data, and pivot when their initial assumptions prove incorrect (Sala et al., 2022, p. 1052).

Types of Pivots: Research has identified various types of pivots that startups may undertake, including product pivots, market pivots, and business model pivots. Each type addresses different aspects of the business strategy and is influenced by specific triggers such as market saturation or competitive pressure (Sohaib et al., 2017, p. 3).

In Corporates

Strategic Realignment: In corporate environments, pivoting refers to a significant realignment of business strategies to adapt to new market realities or competitive landscapes. Pivoting can involve reallocating resources or shifting focus to new business areas (Ayoob et al., 2022, p. 6).

Crisis Response: Corporates may pivot in response to crises, such as economic downturns or technological disruptions, necessitating reevaluating their operational strategies and product offerings (Flechas et al., 2021, p. 895).

Innovation and Growth: Pivoting is not just about crisis response in corporates. It is also a powerful tool for boosting innovation and exploring new growth opportunities. By diversifying product lines or entering new markets, corporates can enhance their competitiveness and inspire a culture of continuous growth (Burnell et al., 2023, p. 12).

Cultural Shift: Pivoting in larger organizations may also entail a cultural shift toward more agile practices, encouraging teams to embrace experimentation and rapid iteration in response to market changes (Ayoob et al., 2022, p. 9).

Pivoting is more than a strategy; it is a lifeline for startups and corporates. It enables them to navigate challenges, survive, and thrive in the ever-changing business landscape. While startups often pivot in response to direct market feedback, corporates may do so for broader strategic realignment or innovation purposes.

7.3 Progressive Pivots and Progress: The Evolution of Airbus and Layer's Collaboration Successes

Airbus's collaboration with Layer provides a compelling example for the crucial element of strong team engagement in overcoming challenges in its progressive pivots.

The collaboration between French aircraft manufacturer Airbus and Layer, a London-based design startup, exemplifies a progressive and dynamic approach to innovation in the aviation industry. Airbus sought to enhance the passenger experience by improving airplane seat design, particularly for long-haul flights. At the heart of this partnership was the ambition to integrate design innovation, ergonomic efficiency, and sustainability, all of which are crucial in the highly competitive and environmentally conscious aerospace market.

Airbus, a global leader in the aerospace sector, partnered with Layer, a cutting-edge design startup led by Benjamin Hubert, to revolutionize airplane seat comfort and efficiency. This collaboration aimed to improve the passenger experience on long-haul flights, where comfort plays a crucial role in customer satisfaction. Hubert's design expertise, coupled with Airbus's technological capabilities, focused on creating adaptable seat designs that could meet diverse passenger needs, including the flexibility to adjust comfort settings via digital controls (Built In, 2024, p. 3).

The evolution of this project has been driven by the dual challenge of making air travel not only more comfortable but also more sustainable. As the market changes, so too must the solutions we provide.

—Benjamin Hubert, founder of Layer

Since its inception, the collaboration between Airbus and Layer has undergone multiple pivots. Beyond numerous product pivots, the collaboration experienced other forms of pivoting, including shifts in business model, target market strategy, and collaborative focus. These changes reflect evolving industry needs and consumer preferences.

The Various Forms of Pivoting

Business Model Pivot: Initially, Layer focused on providing design solutions. However, as sustainability and technological integration became critical, Layer's role expanded beyond mere design to become a key partner in developing sustainable, tech-driven solutions for Airbus. The business model shifted from a project-based design provider to a longer-term strategic collaborator in Airbus's innovation ecosystem (Wilson, 2021, p. 89).

Market Strategy Pivot: While the collaboration began with the aim to improve seating for economy-class passengers on long-haul flights, there was a pivot toward appealing to the growing market of environmentally conscious travelers and airlines seeking to reduce carbon footprints. By adopting sustainable materials and creating ergonomic solutions, Airbus and Layer targeted a wider range of market segments, including airlines promoting eco-friendly flights and customers willing to pay for a greener travel experience (Peeters et al., 2019, p. 378).

Collaborative Focus Pivot: Initially focused on passenger comfort and aesthetics, the collaboration evolved to include digitalization and data analytics through smart seating technologies, allowing real-time passenger preference monitoring. This pivot reflected a broader trend in the aviation industry, where digital transformation is becoming a key driver of competitive advantage (Jones, 2020, p. 25).

Impact of Pivoting on the Business and Bottom Line

The pivots in this collaboration significantly impacted both Airbus's and Layer's business strategies. The adoption of sustainable materials and smart technologies allowed Airbus to differentiate itself in a competitive airline industry increasingly focused on eco-conscious travelers. This strategy gave Airbus a competitive edge, helping secure contracts with airlines prioritizing sustainability. In turn, this benefited Layer by increasing its market credibility and positioning it as an innovative design and technology integration leader.

From a financial perspective, these pivots have contributed to cost reductions for airlines, particularly through the use of lighter, sustainable materials that reduce fuel consumption, thus improving the overall bottom line (Peeters et al., 2019, p. 381). The implementation of smart technologies has also allowed Airbus to explore new revenue streams through data-driven customer insights and in-flight services, creating an added value proposition that could translate into higher profits.

By integrating products, business, sustainability and technology pivots, the Airbus–Layer collaboration has enabled both companies to remain relevant in a rapidly evolving market, securing their long-term growth and competitive positioning.

7.3.1 The Dynamics of Team Engagement in the Airbus and Layer Collaboration

The collaboration between Airbus and Layer illustrates a dynamic process where employee engagement played a central role in navigating multiple pivots. As Airbus, a leader in aerospace, partnered with Layer, a startup specializing in innovative design, both teams faced significant changes in direction—shifting from product innovation to sustainability, ergonomics, and smart technology integration. The engagement of employees from both organizations was essential to managing these shifts and ensuring success.

The dynamics of employee engagement during these pivots revolved around several key factors: leadership adaptability, strengths-based leadership, emotional intelligence, continuous learning, and team empowerment. Each of these elements contributed to building a culture where employees felt valued, motivated, and prepared to contribute meaningfully to the partnership's ongoing evolution.

7.3.2 Employee Engagement Dynamics in Corporate–Startup Pivots

1 **Strengths-Based Leadership and Empowerment:** During the initial stages of the Airbus–Layer collaboration, the focus was on creating adaptable, innovative seat designs for long-haul flights. With their extensive knowledge of aerospace engineering, Airbus employees worked alongside Layer's design specialists. Leadership played a critical role in maximizing the strengths of both teams. Airbus provided its technical and production expertise, while Layer's design team contributed their creative approaches to customer comfort and smart technology (Hubert, 2020, p. 54). Strengths-based leadership ensured that employees from both organizations felt that their unique skills were recognized and valued. For example, Layer's focus on smart textiles allowed Airbus to leverage new technology for in-flight comfort. At the same time, Airbus employees ensured the designs could be scaled and integrated into the airline's broader operations. This collaboration empowered employees to take ownership of their respective contributions, maintaining high engagement throughout the pivot.

2   **Emotional Intelligence in Managing Collaboration Pivots:** Emotional intelligence (EI) was instrumental in managing the different operational cultures of Airbus and Layer. Airbus, being a large corporation, had more rigid structures and long-established processes, while Layer, as a startup, operated with greater agility and creativity. Leaders who exhibited high EI were able to navigate these differences effectively. They fostered an environment where both sides felt heard and respected, even when disagreements arose over design directions or technological integration. The leaders' ability to manage emotions, communicate clearly, and foster empathy contributed to stronger collaboration. When Airbus shifted its focus towards sustainability, Layer's design team needed to adapt their materials and production processes quickly. Airbus leaders facilitated this transition by maintaining open lines of communication, ensuring that employees felt supported as they navigated these changes (Wilson, 2021, p. 90). This high emotional intelligence kept engagement strong, even during uncertain and rapid changes.

3   **Continuous Learning as a Driver of Engagement:** As the Airbus–Layer collaboration evolved, continuous learning became crucial to maintaining employee engagement. The pivot toward sustainability, for instance, required both teams to acquire new knowledge about eco-friendly materials and production methods. Airbus, with its expertise in large-scale manufacturing, had to adapt to using sustainable materials, while Layer needed to ensure that these materials could still meet the ergonomic and comfort standards required for long-haul seating (Peeters et al., 2019, p. 377). Leaders facilitated this learning by encouraging experimentation and providing opportunities for employees to expand their skill sets. This approach kept employees engaged and enhanced their ability to contribute to the partnership's evolving goals. For example, integrating smart technology into the seat design required Airbus engineers to learn about Layer's smart textiles and sensor integration, ensuring that both teams worked cohesively to implement these innovations (Hollywood et al., 2016, p. 39).

4   **Empowering Teams Through Shared Ownership:** A critical element of employee engagement in this collaboration was the sense of shared ownership that leaders instilled in both Airbus and Layer employees. Rather than treating Layer as a subcontractor, Airbus involved the startup as an equal partner, giving its employees a stake in the project's success. This collaborative culture empowered employees at all levels to offer ideas and solutions, which was particularly important during pivots. The importance of shared ownership in enhancing employee engagement and fostering commitment cannot be overstated. For instance, when the collaboration pivoted towards sustainability, both teams participated in brainstorming sessions to find the best materials that would meet environmental standards without sacrificing comfort or functionality. These

sessions were not just about generating ideas but also about making decisions. Airbus and Layer employees had a say in which materials to use, and their input was valued and considered in the final decision-making process. This shared decision-making process increased buy-in from employees and ensured that they remained engaged throughout the pivot (Hubert, 2020, p. 55).

7.3.3 Lessons Learned From Employee Engagement Dynamics in the Airbus–Layer Collaboration

The Airbus–Layer collaboration offers the following valuable insights into the dynamics of employee engagement during corporate-startup pivots:

1   **Engagement Through Empowerment**: Empowering employees by recognizing and leveraging their strengths is key to maintaining engagement, especially when navigating pivots. By ensuring that employees felt their contributions were integral to the collaboration's success, leaders at Airbus and Layer fostered a sense of ownership that kept teams motivated and engaged.
2   **The Importance of Emotional Intelligence**: Leaders who possess high emotional intelligence can better manage the complexities of corporate-startup collaborations. In the Airbus–Layer case, emotionally intelligent leaders helped employees from both organizations work through the cultural and operational differences that often emerge in such partnerships.
3   **Continuous Learning as an Engagement Tool**: By fostering a culture of continuous learning, leaders ensure that employees remain engaged during periods of change. The Airbus–Layer collaboration demonstrated that when employees are given opportunities to develop new skills and contribute to innovative solutions, they are more likely to stay motivated and invested in the project's success.
4   **Shared Ownership Enhances Buy-In**: Employee engagement is most robust when individuals feel they have a stake in the project's outcomes. The collaborative nature of the Airbus-Layer partnership, where both teams contributed to key decisions, fostered a sense of shared ownership that kept engagement levels high throughout the multiple pivots.

The dynamics of employee engagement in the Airbus–Layer collaboration show that empowerment, emotional intelligence, continuous learning, and shared ownership are critical to navigating the complexities of corporate–startup partnerships. These lessons can be applied to similar collaborations to ensure employees remain engaged and motivated even as the partnership evolves.

7.4 Coaching Strategies for Successful Corporate–Startup Pivot

Success depends on more than just aligned goals and shared expertise in the usual complex corporate–startup collaborations for corporate innovation. It requires the strategic application of coaching to drive team engagement and alignment, especially when external factors demand a significant shift in strategy. This case of the NexusTech and MindZen collaboration highlights how coaching directly influences the outcome of a struggling partnership. Faced with the COVID-19 pandemic and shifting consumer demands for personalized wellness solutions, the collaboration initially faltered in its strategic pivot. Through targeted coaching interventions, focusing on team dynamics, emotional intelligence, and courageous conversations, the collaboration regained its footing and excelled in delivering innovative solutions.

7.4.1 Case Study (Composite): NexusTech and MindZen Collaboration

NexusTech, a global technology leader, partnered with MindZen, a wellness startup, to integrate mental health solutions into NexusTech's lifestyle platform. Despite initial enthusiasm, the collaboration struggled to pivot effectively when the COVID-19 pandemic accelerated market shifts. The demand for personalized wellness programs surged, but misalignment and low engagement stalled progress. This case study applies Formulation in Coaching (Lane & Corrie, 2009; Corrie & Lane, 2010; Kovacs, 2016; Corrie & Kovacs, 2017) alongside the GROW model (Whitmore, 2017) to demonstrate how structured coaching interventions in psychological safety, systemic thinking, and goal-setting revitalized the partnership, enabling a successful pivot.

Learning Outcomes

1 Understand how Formulation in Coaching enhances coaching effectiveness.
2 Examine the role of psychological safety and systemic thinking in corporate–startup collaborations.
3 Analyze how coaching frameworks resolve misalignment and challenges in team dynamics.
4 Explore how structured interventions using the GROW model strengthen trust, communication, and leadership engagement during a pivot.
5 Learn how progressive pivoting supports continuous adaptation rather than a one-time pivot.

About the Coach

A leadership development and team coaching specialist was engaged to navigate the complexities of the NexusTech–MindZen partnership. Applying

Formulation in Coaching (Lane & Corrie, 2009, p. 210), the coach implemented systemic strategies to promote psychological safety and encourage reflexive decision-making. Using Clutterbuck's team coaching framework (Clutterbuck, 2013, p. 45), the intervention reinforced collaborative leadership, while the GROW model structured discussions and drove actionable outcomes (Whitmore, 2017, p. 98).

Coaching Contract

The coaching contract established the following three primary objectives:

1 Strengthen team engagement.
2 Improve psychological safety.
3 Develop a structured problem-solving framework.

Systemic thinking guided the intervention, recognizing the interplay between individual and organizational factors in shaping team behavior (Lane & Corrie, 2009, p. 202). Appreciative inquiry (AI) helped surface existing strengths and foster a culture of continuous improvement (Hollywood et al., 2016, p. 35). Structured coaching conversations identified underlying tensions, and the GROW model facilitated goal-setting, reality assessment, options exploration, and commitment to action (Whitmore, 2017, p. 112).

Discussion Questions

1 What challenges might arise when implementing systemic thinking in a corporate–startup partnership, and how can coaches navigate these challenges to drive alignment and innovation?
2 How did the lack of role clarity and poor communication contribute to the initial misalignment between NexusTech and MindZen, and what systemic coaching strategies, if applied earlier, could have been crucial in preventing these issues?
3 How will the emphasis on psychological safety and reflexivity influence team engagement, and what role does appreciative inquiry (AI) play in fostering a culture of continuous improvement?
4 Considering Clutterbuck's team coaching framework and the systemic approach, how can corporate–startup collaborations proactively address potential disengagement and misalignment before they escalate?

7.4.2 Coaching Process

The coach initiated diagnostic sessions to assess engagement levels and systemic challenges. Applying Formulation in Coaching, the teams coconstructed a shared understanding of their collaboration barriers (Lane &

Corrie, 2009, p. 198). The GROW model provided a structured pathway to articulate goals, analyze realities, explore options, and commit to action (Whitmore, 2017, p. 105).

A turning point emerged when teams engaged in structured formulation dialogues and applied the GROW model to create clear action steps. The coach facilitated coaching sessions to help articulate frustrations, identify blind spots, and realign expectations. The coach reinforced psychological safety, empowering individuals to engage in candid discussions and commit to a collective strategic redirection.

Coaching Interventions

The intervention integrated the following three key methodologies:

1 Psychological Safety: The coach created conditions for open dialogue, reducing fear of failure and reinforcing a learning culture (Edmondson, 2019, p. 96).
2 Systemic Thinking: Applying Formulation in Coaching, the team examined organizational interdependencies, shifting focus from isolated challenges to broader systemic patterns (Lane & Corrie, 2009, p. 205).
3 GROW Model Implementation: Structured coaching guided teams through defining Goals, understanding their Reality, generating Options, and committing to Willful action (Whitmore, 2017, p. 120).
4 Progressive Pivoting Application: Teams adapted their strategy incrementally based on real-time feedback, ensuring their pivot remained agile and sustainable.

Progressive Pivoting in Action

The NexusTech–MindZen collaboration exemplifies progressive pivoting, where strategic pivots evolve through continuous adaptation rather than singular shifts. Initially, the team struggled to realign due to unclear communication and misalignment with market needs. Instead of an immediate overhaul, coaching interventions facilitated incremental adjustments based on consumer feedback and market trends. By consistently applying the GROW model, leaders revisited goals, assessed realities, explored new opportunities, and committed to iterative changes (Whitmore, 2017, p. 112). This ongoing cycle ensured that the pivot remained responsive, data-driven, and adaptable to shifting demand.

As clarity increased, NexusTech and MindZen successfully pivoted to personalized wellness programs, leveraging NexusTech's technology infrastructure and MindZen's expertise in content development.

7.4.3 Outcomes and Reflection

The coaching intervention resulted in measurable improvements in leadership cohesion, team alignment, and strategic agility. Leaders developed a stronger sense of accountability, enhancing decision-making and goal execution. Psychological safety was reinforced, leading to more open discussions and collaborative problem-solving. One notable improvement was a 40% increase in team engagement scores, reflecting a shift toward proactive participation and solution-driven mindsets (Edmondson, 2019, p. 110).

Furthermore, internal surveys revealed that 85% of participants felt more confident in navigating uncertainty, citing structured coaching as a catalyst for clarity and innovation (Whitmore, 2017, p. 134). As a direct outcome of improved communication and iterative learning, the teams successfully launched a tailored wellness program that exceeded initial user adoption forecasts by 30% within the first quarter (Hollywood et al., 2016, p. 42).

A key takeaway: Corporate–startup partnerships thrive when coaching interventions blend deep problem analysis with structured execution strategies. Progressive pivoting enabled the teams to shift from reactive adjustments to proactive innovation, ensuring continuous evolution. The collaboration not only achieved its strategic pivot but also cultivated a culture of adaptability and long-term innovation.

Discussion Questions

1   How can the application of Formulation in Coaching, or similar frameworks be used in other challenges in corporate–startup collaborations?
2   How can organizations sustain the GROW model approach beyond coaching sessions?
3   What strategies ensure that psychological safety remains embedded in team dynamics?
4   How can systemic coaching frameworks be scaled to broader corporate partnerships?
5   How can teams sustain progressive pivoting beyond a single transformation?

Conclusion

The NexusTech–MindZen partnership illustrates that strategic pivots demand more than surface-level adjustments; they require a structured, adaptive approach grounded in trust, psychological safety, and systemic learning. Initially hindered by misalignment and disengagement, the collaboration found stability through a coaching framework that integrated the GROW model and Formulation in Coaching. These methodologies provided a structured pathway for clarifying objectives, addressing blind spots, and fostering a culture of accountability.

The intervention's success underscores a critical insight: Pivots should be dynamic, not episodic. Progressive pivoting reframes change as a continuous, responsive process rather than a one-time corrective measure. By embedding systemic thinking and iterative goal-setting, the NexusTech–MindZen team transitioned from reactive problem-solving to proactive innovation, allowing them to align their vision with evolving market demands. Leaders must commit to sustained coaching interventions reinforcing open dialogue, shared purpose, and strategic adaptability. When teams cultivate these conditions, pivots cease to be disruptions and become opportunities for long-term growth and innovation.

Conclusion

Successful corporate–startup pivots depend on engaged teams, strategic alignment, and effective coaching interventions. Pivots are not singular events but ongoing processes requiring adaptability, resilience, and collaborative leadership. Misalignment, disengagement, and resistance to change often derail promising shifts, making leadership and coaching indispensable in navigating these challenges.

The Airbus–Layer case exemplifies how sustained engagement and iterative pivots drive long-term success. Their collaboration evolved beyond seat design innovation to encompass sustainability and digital transformation, demonstrating how continuous adaptation secures competitive advantage. Similarly, the NexusTech–MindZen collaboration illustrates how coaching interventions structured around systemic thinking, Formulation in Coaching, and emotional intelligence transformed a struggling collaboration into a thriving, innovative venture.

The success of these case studies underscores that coaching is not an optional element in pivoting—it is a necessity. The GROW model provided a structured approach to goal-setting, while systemic coaching and Formulation in Coaching ensured alignment between corporate and startup teams. Psychological safety and courageous conversations played critical roles in maintaining team cohesion and engagement throughout the transition.

To execute successful pivots, organizations must embrace coaching as an integral component of change management. Leaders must foster open dialogue, create psychologically safe environments, and empower teams with the tools to navigate uncertainty. Coaching frameworks such as Clutterbuck's team coaching model, appreciative inquiry, the GROW model, and Formulation in Coaching enable teams to transition from reactive adjustments to proactive innovation.

Corporate–startup collaborations thrive when pivots are executed intentionally and guided by strong coaching frameworks. Organizations can navigate transformations effectively by prioritizing engagement, fostering systemic alignment, and embedding a learning culture, ensuring sustainable growth and competitive advantage in an ever-evolving market. The key to successful pivots lies in aligning strategy with team engagement and using coaching as the bridge between vision and execution.

References

Brown, B. (2018). *Dare to lead: Brave work. Tough conversations. Whole hearts.* Random House.

Clutterbuck, D. (2013). *Coaching the team at work.* Nicholas Brealey Publishing.

Edmondson, A. C. (2019). *The fearless organization: Creating psychological safety in the workplace for learning, innovation, and growth.* Wiley.

Goleman, D. (1998). *Working with emotional intelligence.* Bantam Books.

Hollywood, K. G., Blaess, D. A., Santin, C., & Bloom, L. (2016). Holistic mentoring and coaching to sustain organizational change and innovation. *Creighton Journal of Interdisciplinary Leadership, 2*(1), 32–46.

Whitmore, J. (2017). *Coaching for performance: The principles and practice of coaching and leadership* (5th ed.). Nicholas Brealey Publishing.

Chapter 8

An Emergent Role

This chapter serves as a critical lens into the evolving landscape of coaching within corporate innovation. In an era of unprecedented technological advancements, shifting workforce dynamics, and mounting challenges tied to sustainability, coaching has emerged as a decisive force for enabling corporate agility and resilience. This chapter explores how coaching must adapt and expand to address the complex realities faced by organizations striving to innovate in a volatile, uncertain, complex, and ambiguous (VUCA) environment.

As businesses strive to integrate diverse talents and leverage cutting-edge technologies, coaching has transcended traditional methodologies. It now plays a multifaceted role, aligning human potential with technological prowess. Leaders, teams, and innovators need guidance to navigate disruptions, maintain ethical responsibility, and sustain long-term relevance. This evolution underscores the need for coaches to move beyond reactive strategies and become proactive architects of transformative organizational change.

Central to this transformation is the recognition that innovation is not solely a product of technological advances but also a result of human ingenuity and collaboration. Although artificial intelligence (AI) and automation are reshaping industries at an accelerated pace, the success of these tools depends on the people wielding them. Coaching, therefore, becomes indispensable in bridging the gap between technological capabilities and human capacity. By fostering trust, enhancing communication, and cultivating emotional intelligence within teams, coaches help organizations harness the full potential of their innovations.

The concept of "An Emergent Role" also emphasizes the evolving expectations placed upon coaches themselves. Historically, coaching has been a personal, intuitive practice. However, the profession is undergoing a profound transformation with the advent of AI and digital coaching tools. AI-powered coaching avatars and chatbots not only assist human coaches but, in some cases, replace them in specific contexts. This technological encroachment challenges coaches to redefine their unique value proposition—rooted in empathy, ethics, and values-driven interventions. In this chapter, we delve into how coaches can reclaim their relevance by integrating technology into their practice while safeguarding the human essence of coaching.

DOI: 10.4324/9781003469155-12

In addition to technological shifts, workforce demographics are reshaping the coaching landscape. For the first time, five generations coexist within the corporate ecosystem, each shaped by distinct cultural and historical contexts. Generation Z, digital natives influenced by social media, bring a different set of expectations and behaviors to the workplace compared to baby boomers or generation X. Meanwhile, millennials, now ascending into leadership roles, often champion collaborative and purpose-driven approaches that challenge hierarchical structures. The interplay of these generational differences creates a fertile ground for innovation but also presents friction points that require skillful coaching interventions.

By understanding generational dynamics, coaches can unlock the strengths inherent in diversity, fostering an inclusive environment where individuals feel valued for their unique contributions. For instance, millennials' preference for collaborative leadership aligns with open innovation practices, as it promotes external partnerships with startups and other organizations. Similarly, generation Z's adeptness with digital tools can catalyze the adoption of transformative technologies. Coaches play a pivotal role in ensuring that these intergenerational synergies are harnessed to drive innovation.

The role of coaching extends beyond mediating generational differences. In a world grappling with sustainability imperatives and geopolitical uncertainties, organizations are being held accountable for their impact on society and the environment. As such, corporate innovation must transcend profit motives to encompass ethical responsibility and sustainable practices. This shift requires coaches to challenge leaders to think beyond short-term gains and foster a culture of long-term stewardship. By equipping leaders with the tools to navigate ethical dilemmas and balance competing priorities, coaches contribute to creating organizations that are not only innovative but also socially conscious.

Finally, this chapter addresses the critical interplay between emotional intelligence (EI), trust, and communication in innovation ecosystems. Research consistently demonstrates that high-performing teams excel not only in technical skills but also in relational dynamics. For example, Amy Edmondson et al.'s (2001) concept of psychological safety underscores the importance of creating an environment where team members feel secure to voice their opinions, share ideas, and admit mistakes without fear of retribution. Coaches play an instrumental role in fostering such environments, enabling teams to engage in meaningful dialogue and collective problem-solving. Moreover, frameworks such as Patrick Lencioni's (2002) model of team dysfunctions emphasize the foundational role of trust in achieving team cohesion and innovation outcomes.

As the chapter unfolds, we will explore practical strategies for navigating these emerging challenges, including integrating digital tools into coaching practices, fostering intergenerational collaboration, and promoting sustainable innovation. Through case studies and evidence-based insights, we will illuminate how coaches can empower organizations to adapt to a future defined by change. Ultimately, the goal is to equip coaches with the frameworks and tools needed to remain indispensable allies in corporate innovation.

By situating coaching at the nexus of people and technology, this chapter encapsulates the transformative potential of the profession. As we conclude this book, the emergent role of coaching reveals itself not as a static function but as a dynamic force capable of shaping the future of corporate innovation. Coaches who embrace this evolution will not only secure their relevance but also contribute meaningfully to creating organizations that thrive in complexity and uncertainty.

Key Takeaways

- **People and Technology:** Corporate innovation thrives at the intersection of human ingenuity and technology, requiring a balance between technical advancements and the capacity of individuals and teams to utilize them effectively.
- **Coaches as Connectors:** Coaches play a critical role in aligning organizational goals with individual potential, enabling teams to navigate challenges and capitalize on opportunities.
- **Interpersonal Relationships:** Strong relationships founded on respect, trust, and open communication form the bedrock of effective teamwork and drive innovation.
- **Psychological Safety:** Creating a safe environment where team members can share ideas, admit mistakes, and engage in open discussions is vital for innovation to flourish.
- **Trust as a Foundation:** Trust is essential for cohesive team dynamics, fostering collaboration and empowering teams to work toward common goals.
- **Generational Diversity:** The multigenerational workforce offers unique perspectives, and effective coaching bridges these differences to promote inclusivity and collaboration.
- **Millennial Leadership:** Millennial leaders' focus on collaboration and empowerment aligns well with the needs of modern innovation and open innovation strategies.
- **Emotional Intelligence:** Managing interpersonal complexities, enhancing decision-making, and building resilience is strengthened by emotional intelligence.
- **AI in Coaching:** The integration of AI in coaching enhances efficiency, offers data-driven insights, and broadens access to coaching resources.
- **Ethical AI Practices:** Responsible use of AI in coaching ensures data security, confidentiality, and fairness, safeguarding client trust.
- **Values-Based Coaching:** Aligning individual and organizational priorities through values-driven approaches creates meaningful connections and purpose-led leadership.

- **Coaching Supervision:** Structured supervision improves professional standards and ensures continuous development among coaches for better outcomes.
- **Adaptability in Coaching:** Future coaching strategies must emphasize flexibility, cross-disciplinary collaboration, and the integration of digital tools to meet evolving needs.
- **Sustainability and Ethics:** Corporate innovation must incorporate sustainability and ethical considerations, with coaches guiding leaders to balance profitability and societal impact.
- **The Evolving Role of Coaching:** Coaching continues to evolve alongside technological and societal shifts, emphasizing the importance of lifelong learning and purpose-driven approaches.

8.1 Decisive Factors for Corporate Innovation

As we look ahead into the future of corporate innovation, two decisive factors rise to the forefront: people and technology. These elements are not new in their significance, but their convergence creates a dynamic shift that will define the next era of business.

To thrive, organizations must recalibrate their approach, placing a stronger emphasis on people. The potential of technology, no matter how sophisticated, depends entirely on the ability of individuals and teams to harness it effectively. The real innovation will occur here, at the intersection of human capability and technological advancement.

The growing complexity of today's business environment demands not only new skills but also new strategies to unlock these capabilities. Corporate innovation can no longer depend solely on technical advancements; it must invest deeply in the human side of the equation. Coaching will play an even more pivotal role in guiding leaders, teams, and innovators through this transformation. Emerging business imperatives such as ethics, intellectual property management, sustainability, and the looming influence of Generation Alpha (Kasasa, 2021) demand faster decision-making, greater agility, and a clear sense of direction. Leaders will need coaching to navigate these challenges, pivoting quickly where necessary and collaborating strategically to drive progress.

The challenge is exacerbated by the multigenerational workforce that can be found in any typical startup or corporate setting. Distinct historical, cultural, and technological contexts shape employees hailing from each generation. Hence, each generation brings a distinct characteristic that influences their beliefs and culture to the workplace. The attempt here is not to generalize each individual or to box them into each generation. As practicing coaches, we believe everyone is unique and possesses a transformative power that only they can unlock within them. However, looking at the workforce from the generational workforce's lens can help shape our approach to coaching, especially in innovation coaching.

According to Kasasa (2021), generational cohorts are defined loosely by the birth of the year and not current age, with the oldest cohort being the baby boomers, followed by generation X (gen X), generation Y (millennials), generation Z (gen Z) and the most recent cohort, generation alpha.

Generation	Birth Years	Major Influences
Baby boomers	1946–1964	Post–World War II prosperity
Generation X (gen X)	1965–1980	Rise of technology marked by the advent of the internet
Millennials (gen Y)	1981–1996	Internet explosion
Generation Z (gen Z)	1997–2012	Social media influence
Generation alpha	2013 onward	Rapid technological advancements (artificial intelligence, computing power)

The multigenerational workforce is typically comprised of gen X, gen Y, and gen Z, with gen Z being the latest to enter the workforce. The oldest gen Z would be in their late 20s at the time of writing, bringing a different culture to work. Influenced by the internet explosion and social media influence, gen Z is likely to detail their personal and work lives on social media platforms.

On the other hand, millennials, who were shaped by the arrival of the internet is now entering leadership positions. In their mid-40s, many would-be leaders in large corporations or their own companies, bring with them a preferred leadership style that is remarkably different from gen X.

Medyanik (2016) identifies the following leadership styles favored by Millennials:

1   **Collaborative Leadership:** Millennial leaders prioritize teamwork and collaboration. They also tend to seek consensus regarding decision-making, sharing responsibility, and fostering a sense of community.
2   **Empowerment:** Millennial leaders believe in empowering their followers to perform. While they will continue to set deadlines and expectations, they provide their followers with a high degree of autonomy to accomplish them.
3   **Strong Listening Skills:** Millennial leaders are known to have strong listening skills that will allow them to foster a shared community. They are also prone to use this skill to motivate their followers or employees.
4   **Lead by Example:** Millennial leaders will want to lead by example. This is understandable as they tend to want to use a team approach. The best leaders are those who inspire their followers with the word "come" rather than "go."

What is then the implication of such findings to the context of innovation and collaboration? It does augur well for both scenarios, as shown next:

1   **Innovation:** As significant autonomy is given to the team, the opportunity for innovation to occur will increase. Innovation is often seen as an outcome of a creative process. While true, this creative process requires a certain amount of autonomy and freedom of expression among the team members.
2   **Diversity:** With a more collaborative approach, the millennial leaders will be able to derive the collective innovative prowess of all the team members. This is especially true for introverts, who are often seen as more strategic in their thinking but are less likely to voice their ideas as easily as an extrovert. Research has also indicated that introverts tend to engage in deep thinking and introspection, which can lead to unique and innovative ideas (Dannar, 2016).
3   **Open Innovation:** With strong listening skills, there might be opportunities to engage with external open innovation opportunities as these leaders will be open to listening to what an external party offers, such as a startup. What resources startups lack, they make it up with unique ideas and innovation.

In short, the diversity of the intergenerational workforce, led by a more collaborative leader in the form of a millennial, will result in a more diverse range of responses to innovation challenges and winning the market. The pace of innovation, especially in a startup, is so dynamic and fast that it often requires an equally fast response, whether to pivot or repurpose the innovation.

This also augurs well with the open innovation collaboration between these two highly different cultures. Open innovation requires a different approach to allow two contrasting entities to work together for a common goal. This requires superior communication between the two teams and a leader capable of building relationships with these two diverse teams.

Henceforth, coaches can help such teams to collaborate by focusing on building relationships.

8.2 Building Relationships

In the words of Clutterbuck (2020), "pretty much every study of team effectiveness identifies the quality of interpersonal relationships as a critical component." While it may not be necessary for each team member to "like" everyone, it is critical that the team respect, trust, and be open with each other.

With the diversity of the generational workforce in both the startups and their collaborating corporates, coaches need to focus on helping both team members build stronger relationships that will not undermine teamwork, especially in a highly disruptive and transient innovation process. Teamwork is critical as the team needs to respond to the disruptive nature of their work—a product being innovated can be made obsolete when a larger startup or corporate incorporates it as a new feature in their offerings. The team must come together to respond to this threat, whether to proceed or to pivot.

8.2.1 The Relationship Factor

Clutterbuck (2020) has identified the following areas of relationship that would require attention:

Respect: There are two main aspects here that would need the team's attention: valuing someone for their expertise and competence and valuing them as a human being. In valuing someone for their expertise, the younger generations, especially gen Z and younger, are recognized for their technology competence but may be seen as inexperienced. At the same time, the older generations will be acknowledged for their experience but may not be respected regarding technology.

The key to building this mutual respect among team members, especially of different generational compositions, is to drill down to the component that made us all human: the values we all hold dear. Understanding each other's values will help us get to know one another better, as it will allow us to understand what is important and is of priority to each other.

Coaches can encourage the team members to first list their top five priorities, then split them into pairs and for each pair to compare their cards. If there is a match, then the pair can share why they hold that value and give examples from their experiences. If there are no matches, the pair can each choose a value that is important to them and hold a dialogue to see if these two can complement each other. This coaching conversation is then open to the group for a dialogue on values and how everyone can support each other in upholding their values.

Psychological Safety: Do team members feel safe voicing their opinions, sharing ideas, and admitting mistakes? Admitting mistakes is essential in any innovation process, as mistakes can sometimes provide a pivot to an entirely new innovative product. Edmondson et al. (2001) found that in a study of 16 surgical teams moving from open heart to keyhole surgery, the success of adapting to the new procedure correlated to a higher degree of psychological safety. The high degree of psychological safety has allowed team members to voice opinions, suggestions, and ideas without fear of looking stupid. Therefore, we can safely say that creating this psychological safety net is crucial, especially in an innovation process.

Some of Edmondson's conclusions that are good for consideration follow:

- Coaching by a team leader is associated with team learning and psychological safety. It may be worthwhile to train the team leader with coaching skills.

- Team learning is associated with a "shared belief that one will not be blamed by other team members, who can be counted on to help each other and who are not punitive." Creating such a team culture will foster the giving and acceptance of constructive feedback.

Clutterbuck (2020) suggests that one way to help a team grow in psychological safety is to acclimate the team to openness. He suggested starting awards that celebrate "best mistakes" and for the team leader to win the prize from time to time!

Trust: In his book, *The Five Dysfunctions of a Team*, Patrick Lencioni places trust at the foundation of his pyramid. In other words, the core issue with any dysfunctional team is the basic lack of trust. Trust has also been shown to correlate positively with performance in a team and negatively with anxiety and stress (Costa et al., 2001).

Trust is even more critical when two teams (startup and corporate) in culture and composition converge to collaborate on innovation. In the previous chapters, an attempt has been made to guide coaches in helping these different teams build trust through innovation. Herein, we will introduce a behavioral framework created by Dr Paul Zak (Zak, 2017) under the acronym OXYTOCIN to help the team build trust:

Ovation: Recognition for those who meet or exceed goals
eXpectation: Design stretched challenges (difficult but achievable) and hold colleagues accountable to reach them.

Yield: Enable employees to complete their tasks as they deem fit.
Transfer: Give employees autonomy to self-manage themselves.
Openness: Share information broadly
Caring: Build relationships with colleagues intentionally.
Invest: Promote employees' personal and professional growth.
Natural: Behave authentically and ask for help.

Communication: Research has shown that communication is an important factor in team effectiveness. Pentland (2012), in a study that tracked team members' interaction continuously for several weeks, found that high-performing teams' interaction frequency is much higher than lower-performing ones. Peatland has also defined the following five characteristics of a team that communicates well together:

- Everyone talks and listens in roughly equal measure. Contributions are kept short.
- Members maintain a high level of eye contact while their conversations and gestures are energetic.

- Members communicate directly with one another as well as with the team leader.
- Members carry on back-channel or side conversations within the team.
- Members periodically break away from the team, explore outside the team, and return with information to share.

However, the key is how we can help the team achieve those communication characteristics. What are some of the interventions a coach could introduce that could catalyze the development of such a communicative team? The key lies in helping the team to have dialogues or "dialogic conversations" (Clutterbuck & Megginson, 2004).

This dialogic conversation goes beyond transactional or instructional conversations, such as making requests or giving an order. Clutterbuck and Megginson (2004) categorized them into seven different types as follows:

1 **Social Dialogue:** These are social conversations that lead to relationship-building between individuals. The point of these conversations is meant to help one get to know the other individual as a person and not only as a team member at work.
2 **Technical Dialogue:** These conversations are mostly work related, namely, about processes or policies at work. The purpose is to help each other complete the tasks at hand.
3 **Tactical Dialogue:** These conversations help with overcoming issues at hand. Mostly, it will be work related but could also be at a personal level.
4 **Strategic Dialogue:** These conversations help with looking at issues from a broader perspective, helping people to have a vision of what they desire the change to be.
5 **Dialogue for Self-Insights:** These conversations enable people to have a better understanding of themselves, to understand their fear and their limitations, and to help them search for answers which are buried within themselves.
6 **Dialogue for Change:** A team conversation to help the team adapt the information received and adapt it into a collective response.
7 **Integrative Dialogue:** These conversations aim to help people find clarity about who they are and to find their place in the world. Clutterbuck (2020) postulate that at the team level, this sort of conversation enables the integration of personal and collective purpose.

The relationship remains the building blocks in innovation as it is, after all, still a human endeavor underpinned by relationships and a sense of shared purpose, shared vision, and shared dreams.

Meanwhile, technology continues to reshape the landscape with rapid advancements. The question for businesses is not only which technologies to adopt but how to implement them in a way that complements broader goals such as sustainability and ethical responsibility. In a world marked by geopolitical tensions, climate challenges, and shifting demographics, corporations must innovate in ways that align with these emerging imperatives. This will require collaboration at an unprecedented level, with corporate innovation relying heavily on internal and external partnerships.

The demand for new coaching strategies is apparent. Leaders will need guidance on building teams capable of responding to technological disruptions while upholding the values of ethics, sustainability, and social responsibility. This chapter will continue to explore the emerging role of coaching innovation in this evolving landscape, focusing on the critical balance between people and technology and the strategies that will enable corporate innovation to thrive in a future defined by change.

8.3 People–Technology Convergence

8.3.1 AI—the Transformative Technology

At the point of writing, artificial intelligence (AI) has taken a giant leap into our world, threatening to disrupt almost every industry, including coaching and innovation. As insinuated by the name AI, it does, in the nature of its construct, contain a certain amount of intelligence.

What do we mean by that? One of our human intelligence strengths is our ability to recognize patterns; it is easy for us to pick up Romance languages, such as French, Spanish, and Italian, once we learn one of the three, as they all share the same grammatical pattern construct. Similarly, it is easy for us to learn how to pick the odd ones out as we could quickly pick out the "ugly duckling" among the rest of the ducklings.

However, a computer program such as AI cannot do that, as a computer program solves problems using a logical, step-by-step method. This is now known as "classical" or "symbolic" AI, the prevalent paradigm from the 1950s to the 1990s. Classical AI is essentially a logical reasoning program designed by a human programmer using symbols and rules to represent concepts and the relationship between these concepts. A famous example would be Deep Blue, the groundbreaking chess-playing computer developed by IBM, which beat the then reigning world chess champion, Gary Kasparov, in a rematch. Conceived initially in 1985 at Carnegie Mellon University, the final version utilized a parallel architecture with 256 processors, enabling it to search "200 million chess positions per second" (Wikipedia, n.d.).

However, as problems become more complex, even with greater computing power, it is too cumbersome to write a programming language to solve them. Today, Deep Blue has been retired to the Museum of American History and the Computer History Museum. Each of the museums received one of the two racks that made up Deep Blue (Wikipedia, n.d.).

All this changed when we were able to teach the computer program to learn to perform tasks on its own without the need for human programming. Computer scientists call this *machine learning*. Machine learning involves using data sets to train AI models, including models that mimic the human brain, known as "artificial neural networks."

These data are differentiated into the following three major types:

1   **Training Data:** Used to train machine learning to perform task accurately.
2   **Validation Data:** Used to assess the accuracy of AI in processing the training data during the learning phase.
3   **Test Data:** Used to test the accuracy of the training (DK, 2024).

In short, computers are now able to learn from information. All the computers, or more explicitly, the AI, need are just to be fed and to be trained with information, or, more specifically, data. Nigel Toon (2024), in his explorative book, *How AI Thinks: How We Built It, How It Can Help Us, and How We Can Control It*, wrote, "Having machines learn from information—rather than just telling them what to do, step by step, in a program—unleashes perhaps the most important breakthrough in computing since the very first electronic computers."

AI is now generative and capable of creating new content, whether it is text, images, or even music, based on the data on which the AI is trained. AI is now known as *generative AI*. At the time of writing, generative AI is used to create images from text, videos from text, new text based on existing text files, and more. It is truly a transformational technology that is disrupting every industry in a way that changes how things are being done.

With stronger computing powers, more complex models were made possible, including the ChatGPT, essentially a version of the Large Language Model (LLM). LLMs are large computational models consisting of trillions of parameters trained on billions of data elements (Kasneci et al., 2023). These models used complex and advanced techniques in natural language processing (NLP) to understand and produce highly accurate human language text based on input prompts.

LLMs can be used not only to produce text but also to summarize multiple documents, create stories based on certain styles of famous authors, make suggestions for mundane activities such as cleaning the house, and even interact with a human in a multilingual conversation.

8.3.2 The Convergence: Applying AI in Coaching

Yes, AI is now capable of "listening" and engaging in a dialogue with a client. Based on the prompts, the response will vary. This is highly similar to a coaching conversation. A coach's biggest asset is the ability to hold a transformative conversation whereby the client can discover, deep down with themselves, the answers that they were searching for. A generative AI can fill this role efficiently if the client can provide reasonably accurate prompts to the AI.

Nevertheless, with this new capability, AI has begun to change the way coaching sessions are being conducted. AI avatars of coaches are being created, whereby the AI is trained to mimic an actual coach, which encompasses the coach's style and thinking process, then deployed to replace the actual coach, to be used when the coach is not physically present to engage with the client. You, as a coach, are now capable of running sessions during the day and then proceeding to let your avatar replace you when you go to bed. The AI avatar has allowed the coach to be on standby 24/7 to serve the client. Without going into details on ethics and compliance issues, this is truly a remarkable feat for any coach.

Terblanche et al. (2024) envisioned four new main areas where AI can play a role in organizational coaching. The four main areas are coaching emulation, coaching support, coach education, and coaching data analysis.

1   **Coach Emulation:** A replacement of a coach, especially with the use of chatbots. Terblanche et al. (2022) have demonstrated in this comparative study that AI coaching chatbots are quite effective in certain coaching contexts. Chatbots can be seen as a simpler version of AI coaching and possibly deployed as the initial contact point for the client without the presence of the coach.

 Another advantage of chatbots is that "they can collect data with each client interaction" (Terblanche, 2024). These data can be analyzed to understand the coachee, especially when the transformative coaching takes place or when the client reaches the "aha" moment. In an organizational format, these data can be used even for team coaching and leader coaching. The question is, how do you do this ethically?

2   **Coach Support:** AI can function as a supporting tool by removing administrative work from the coach during the entire coaching process. Prior to the beginning of the coaching process, AI can be utilized to help with matching and screening coaches for their clients. Matching coaches to their counterparts is highly tedious work, but it is critical that it is done correctly. Next, during the coaching engagement, AI can be used to check in on the clients during the "lull time" in between coaching sessions or even to help the client work on self-reflection until the next appointed session. Similarly, the AI can be used to extend the coaching interaction postengagement by functioning as a tool to help the client self-reflect and plot ahead.

3   **Coaching Skills Development:** Coaching sessions can be recorded for AI to analyze and provide an assessment of the skills of the coach compared to a standardized competency framework. It can also function as a developmental coach by helping the coach focus on areas of weakness through the analysis of the video of the previous session.

4 **Analysis of Coaching Intervention Post Facto:** This is essentially a gathering of data on coaching interventions, which were traditionally captured by coaches through notes taken down during coaching. There is a wealth of information here that could help not only the client but also the coach and the paying employer. Terblanche et al. (2024) postulated that "human coaching data could be submitted for AI analysis to detect trends and patterns not only within one client intervention but across the entire organisation's coaching interventions." This will potentially unlock a lot of potential within the organization and, at the same time, better coaching intervention as a whole for the organization. An example would be the deployment of team coaching after analyzing such data.

Real-World Examples of AI Integration in Corporate Coaching

I UNILEVER'S USE OF AI FOR LEADERSHIP DEVELOPMENT

Unilever, a multinational consumer goods company, implemented an AI-based coaching platform to enhance its leadership training programs. The company used CoachHub, an AI-enabled digital coaching platform, to provide personalized coaching for its employees across various levels of the organization. Through this platform, Unilever aimed to democratize access to coaching by offering one-on-one virtual coaching sessions. The platform leveraged advanced data analytics to assess employees' leadership styles, behavioral tendencies, and growth areas. It matched employees with professional coaches based on their individual needs and goals, ensuring optimal alignment between the coachee and the coach. This approach accelerated the leadership development process, enabling leaders to adopt inclusive decision-making and improve team dynamics. The integration of AI streamlined the administrative tasks traditionally associated with coaching, allowing Unilever's leadership coaches to focus on substantive, value-driven engagements (CoachHub, 2023, p. 14).

2 GOOGLE'S WHISPER PROJECT

Google launched the Whisper Project to improve managerial effectiveness using a combination of AI and human coaching. This initiative aimed to address team dynamics and leadership challenges by equipping managers with actionable insights. The program employed AI tools to analyze communication patterns, meeting structures, and feedback mechanisms within teams.

For instance, the AI flagged instances where communication styles hindered collaboration or where team members were excluded from discussions. Human coaches then worked with managers to refine their approaches, balancing technical problem-solving with relational leadership. The program's success lies in its ability to combine data-driven recommendations with human insights, allowing managers to cultivate psychological safety and trust within their teams (Edmondson et al., 2001, p. 685).

3 PWC'S MY+ TRANSFORMATION INITIATIVE

PricewaterhouseCoopers (PwC) introduced the My+ transformation initiative, which incorporated AI to revolutionize employee coaching and professional development. The program employed AI algorithms to create tailored growth plans based on employees' aspirations, skill gaps, and performance data.

AI systems provided continuous feedback, tracked progress, and suggested specific actions to meet career milestones. In parallel, human coaches provided nuanced guidance, addressing challenges the AI identified but could not resolve entirely. For example, when employees struggled with interpersonal conflicts or team integration, coaches stepped in to facilitate value-based dialogues. By harmonizing AI's efficiency with the empathetic capabilities of human coaching, PwC's initiative enhanced workforce engagement and performance (Terblanche et al., 2022, p. 12).

The key to the application of all the suggested functions of AI is the guarantee of privacy and an ethical methodology to draw the necessary data for AI training and deployment. The coaching industry may require an additional technology approach to accreditation to safeguard the use of such AI and to guarantee the safety of the clients.

8.4 The Future of AI Coaching

The future of AI coaching remains to be seen, but what is clear is that the enablement of AI in coaching is racing at an almost breakneck speed. ChatGPT was publicly launched on November 30, 2022, and by January 2023, in a matter of 2 months of its launch, it had garnered over 100 million users. And as of August 2024, ChatGPT has reached approximately 200 million weekly active users. ChatGPT has become the fastest-growing consumer software application in modern history (Wiggers et al., 2024).

The evidence clearly points to a keen interest in AI, and this is also the case with coaching clients, as proven by Terblanche et al. (2024), which showed that clients welcome the use of AI coaching assistants, provided that their human coaches endorse it. This demand will only continue to grow as AI continues to roll out better and more complex solutions. The coaching industry and coaches cannot and must not ignore this nascent technology that is changing all industries across the board.

Another key consideration is the speed of technology that is bringing new capabilities to AI coaching that will soon surpass the cognitive capability of a coach. The AI scientists identify this as the point of "singularity" (DK, 2024), whereby, at a point in time, AI would have become as smart as the human who built it and would be capable of building its own AI. If and when we reach the point of singularity in the future, we will no longer be able to predict the outcomes of not only coaching but also our lives.

Herein lies an opportunity for the coaching industry to set the tone for how AI coaching can be developed in the future with guidelines and frameworks from established professional bodies such as the European Mentoring and Coaching Council (EMCC). It is imperative for coaches and such professional bodies to guide AI developers who may not be as informed on the ethical and competency considerations of coaching based on the foundation of strong science.

The coaching industry should expand its stakeholders beyond just the coaches and the clients but also technologists such as AI scientists, data scientists or even any individual who may be using AI to create applications for AI in coaching. There is an urgent need to create this platform for dialogue and to convince stakeholders who are not familiar with professional coaching standards to be part of the conversation.

8.4.1 Why Is That the Case?

ChatGPT and other Large Language Models (LLM) have democratized access to AI technology, enabling individuals without technical expertise and coaching expertise to create applications in coaching. An example would be Coach Marlee (getmarlee.com), an AI coach that utilizes ChatGPT to provide tailored coaching by understanding user goals and emotions through advanced sentiment analysis and intent recognition. While this is a welcomed technological advancement, concerns about correct use and compliance with ethical and privacy needs remain unresolved.

The clients who use such AI applications would also need to be protected as they will be given the power to chart their own coaching needs by just prompting the AI application. Again, while this is a tremendous leap forward in empowering coaching clients to tailor advice that fits their situation or growth process, compliance with ethics is contentious.

In conclusion, it is best that the coaching industry acknowledges that AI has become an integral part of the industry and an important technology advancement that clients demand. Now, apart from the involvement of professional bodies in setting standards, what are some approaches coaches could adopt to strengthen their coaching offerings? Would a new coaching framework based on values be an appropriate response?

8.4.2 A New Approach to Coaching

The argument today is probably no longer about the effectiveness or the strength of AI, but rather, it is whether AI is a tool or an agent. Many continue to argue that AI is just a tool to be applied and controlled by a human master. But if you think deeper and reflect quietly without prejudice on the capability of AI today, you'll realize that it already has agency.

What is agency or to have agency? Agency is the ability to take action and to choose what action to take. An example would be ChatGPT. Humans enter a prompt, and the results of that prompt, from the choice of words, the choice of facts, and the choice of references, are all dependent on ChatGPT. This ability is the most basic function that almost all LLMs can do with ease. The argument on the accuracy of what is produced or the fact that "hallucination" happens does not negate the fact that the AI has agency in producing the response to the prompt.

The same argument is valid for AI in coaching. At the time of writing, most AI coaches, be it a chatbot or an avatar, can hold a coaching conversation with a client without the need for human intervention. Companies offering such services are already prevalent in the market and are looking into bringing such AI coaches into the mainstream. A simple search on Google returns significant results for such AI companies.

8.4.3 Coaching Strategies and Practices

With the inevitable emergence of AI into the coaching industry, there is an urgent need to relook at some of the coaching practices to ensure that AI is a positive disruption to the human coach. Professional bodies could begin to evaluate a new competency model or approach that will encompass AI in coaching based on data. Engagement with clients, especially organizations, is urgent and critical for the adoption of such new coaching approaches.

We will examine some coaching processes and practices that could be adapted to meet the new challenges.

8.4.3.1 Values-Based Coaching

Values underpin beliefs and ethics, values motivate action to achieve goals, values exceed precise actions or situations, and values function as standards linked to affect action (Schwartz, 1992). Schwartz (2012) defined *values* as "trans-situational goals varying in importance that serve as a guiding principles in a person or a group." Values are guiding principles that individuals use to develop their goals and guide their decision-making towards that goal.

Values are also seen as strengths; Peterson and Seligman (2004) created the popular Values in Action Inventory of Strengths Survey (VIA-IS) to classify character strengths and virtues. The use of strength-based coaching in congruence with values has shown to be generally validated in positive psychology interventions for well-being (Fouracres & van Nieuwerburgh, 2020).

While values-based coaching is showing promise as an effective coaching method, research focusing on this area is lacking. One of the main reasons could be that coaching for values remains an ambitious concept, unlike the more goal-oriented coaching we are all familiar with.

However, the advent of AI may compel us to relook at this methodology as a more appropriate intervention in conjunction with the use of AI in coaching. Coaching in congruence in values is still a very human endeavor, a matter that speaks to the heart of the clients, not something that could be easily drawn out from data.

Van Nieuwerburgh and Allaho (2018) found that the "Ershad" coaching framework offers a suitable application of coaching for value from an Islamic perspective. This framework allows coaches to align their practice with Islamic teaching and culture and serve individuals from the Muslim faith. This is a marked departure from the standard practice of coaching, which is goal oriented and more individualistic in nature. Based on the "Ershad" framework, Allaho and van Nieuwerburgh (2017) then proceeded to develop the concept of coaching for alignment (CFA). Combining the concepts from "Ershad" and positive psychology, CFA attempts to mirror the coaching framework of allowing the client, also identified as a learner, to consider positive intentions over goals. Succinctly, to consider values over objective goals as the main aim of coaching intervention.

Patel and van Nieuwerburgh (2022) conducted research to investigate the insights of coaches' experience with using the CFA framework. Their research indicated that the coaches felt empowered as a result of a values-based approach to coaching. Some comments were that "coaching for values was a natural way to coach and were empowered by experiencing the model as an authentic way to coach" (Patel and van Nieuwerburgh, 2022).

By adopting values-based coaching, the coaching program could go beyond the mechanical conversation designed through the framework, which would have been "studied and mimicked" by AI. This form of coaching conversations derived the "aha" moment, or when the client unlocked something within themselves from the human relationship with the coach driven by values, the "what" behind the intention.

8.4.3.2 Coaching Supervision

Coaching supervision is an essential practice within the coaching profession. It is recognized as a form of self-development for professional coaches. International Coaching Federation (ICF; n.d.) defined coaching supervision as a "collaborative learning practice" that allows the coaches to reflect on their successes and failures in a safe space. It is a structured process where more senior coaches guide the supervised coaches in a reflective dialogue. The aim is not only for the coach to self-develop but also to ensure higher quality services will be provided to clients in the future. Hence, coaching supervision is seen as a separate skill that extends beyond coaching, and supervisors must be accredited first.

The European Mentoring and Coaching Council (EMCC) also requires its accredited coaches to engage in regular supervision to maintain their credentials, highlighting the importance of such supervision in the profession. In short, supervision is a mechanism that allows coaches to enhance their skills, ensure ethical practices, and provide emotional support to the coaches.

This structured approach not only aids coaches in navigating complex client dynamics but also promotes a culture of check and balance to ensure professionalism in the industry. Quality of coaching is also maintained through the coaches' self-reflection, ensuring that the best quality of coaching is offered to clients.

The question that begs an answer now is: Who supervises AI coaches? An even more important question is, what is AI coaching supervision? Are there standards and frameworks in place that could help AI coaches or AI in coaching self-reflect or self-regulate so that they can provide better quality coaching to clients?

Even the supervisor of these AI coaches or AI in coaching has to be defined. Do they need technology skills for the supervision? Would working with a technology company suffice to supplement the supervisory work? Would the clients agree with AI coaches who are not supervised, or would they, instead, the supervision be done from a technology angle?

Plenty of work still needs to be done to bring this new form of coaching to the fore. The industry needs to fill these voids urgently and provide guidance on moving AI forward in the coaching industry.

8.4.3.3 Ethical Considerations

One of the biggest concerns at the moment with AI is its ethical use. While standards and policies are still being developed, AI has raced ahead with new capabilities and continues challenging the limitations of existing ethical codes. An example would be the concern of biases in the data being used to train AI. What ethical frameworks can AI companies follow to ensure that the AI model being trained is not diffusing cultural, racial or gender biases? The absence of an AI ethical code will hamper the adoption of AI in coaching.

Data privacy and security is also another genuine concern that must be addressed. As coaching conversations are continued "fed" into AI, there is a risk that such data may be accessed unlawfully, intentionally or not. What guarantee can be given to clients that their sharing with the AI coach is safe?

Confidentiality, after all, is the key hallmark of coaching. Coaches often provide a disclaimer that they would keep all conversations secret and will not even share with the client's employer unless it is in a life-threatening situation.

As with supervision, new stakeholders need to be involved in creating such an ethical framework. These stakeholders may include data scientists, AI scientists, data security experts, coaches, and clients. A more expansive stakeholder familiar with technology could be vital in crafting a practical framework in view of AI adoption.

A collaborative approach must be adopted to allow stakeholders, especially the technology experts, to understand the art of coaching. These diverse professionals must be allowed to contribute ideas and feedback to enrich the framework and promote a sense of ownership.

AI's rapid advancement has enabled us to achieve more with fewer resources and presents a valuable opportunity to reflect on and update existing ethical frameworks for coaching. The new framework must align with the technological development that is currently affecting the coaching industry.

To safeguard coaching's core principles, organizations like the International Coaching Federation emphasize embedding confidentiality, nonjudgment, and mutual respect into all interactions, whether mediated by humans or machines (ICF, n.d.). These principles must extend into the digital domain.

Conclusion

The evolving landscape of corporate innovation demands a reimagined approach to coaching that embraces technological advances while preserving the core of human connection. This chapter, "An Emergent Role," has outlined how the intersection of people and technology creates unparalleled opportunities for innovation yet also presents complex challenges that require nuanced coaching strategies. As we conclude this exploration, several key themes emerge, underscoring the indispensable role of coaching in navigating this transformation.

Corporate innovation thrives on the ability to integrate diverse perspectives and leverage cutting-edge technologies. However, technology alone does not drive innovation; it is the people who wield these tools that determine their success. Coaches stand as crucial intermediaries, bridging the gap between technological potential and human capability. They guide leaders and teams in building the trust, emotional intelligence, and collaboration necessary to unlock creativity and achieve sustained progress. As Amy Edmondson's work on psychological safety demonstrates, teams excel when they operate in environments where they feel secure to express ideas and experiment without fear of judgment (Edmondson et al., 2001, p. 685).

At the heart of this coaching paradigm lies the need to cultivate relationships. In corporate–startup collaborations, intergenerational teams, and open innovation ecosystems, trust and communication remain pivotal. Patrick Lencioni's framework of team dysfunctions highlights trust as the foundation for effective teamwork (2002, p. 27). Coaches play a vital role in fostering this trust, enabling diverse groups to align around shared goals and work synergistically. By facilitating open dialogue and encouraging authentic interactions, coaches reassure teams that they can navigate the complexities of today's innovation landscape with confidence.

The generational diversity within the workforce further underscores the importance of tailored coaching approaches. Millennials' preference for collaborative leadership and generation Z's technological fluency offer distinct advantages, yet these strengths can be harnessed only through intentional coaching that bridges generational divides. Coaches must help organizations recognize the value of each generation's contributions while mitigating friction points. By doing so, they empower leaders to create inclusive cultures that harness the collective intelligence of their teams.

Integrating artificial intelligence into coaching practices adds another layer of complexity and opportunity. As AI tools become more sophisticated, they offer coaches the ability to augment their work, streamline processes, and extend their reach. However, this technological shift also raises ethical considerations. AI in coaching must align with principles of confidentiality, data security, and fairness. Coaches must advocate for the responsible development and deployment of these tools, ensuring they enhance rather than diminish the human essence of coaching.

Ethical considerations extend beyond technology to encompass broader organizational responsibilities. Corporate innovation today is inextricably linked to sustainability and social accountability. Coaches must challenge leaders to consider the long-term implications of their decisions, balancing profitability with ethical stewardship. By encouraging values-driven leadership, coaches contribute to organizations that not only innovate but also act as responsible corporate citizens, making the audience feel the weight of their responsibility.

As we look to the future, the coaching profession itself must evolve. Coaches must embrace lifelong learning to stay abreast of technological advancements and emerging trends. They must also expand their skill sets to include the facilitation of cross-disciplinary collaborations, the integration of digital tools, and the cultivation of adaptive leadership qualities. Professional bodies, such as the European Mentoring and Coaching Council (EMCC), have a crucial role in establishing frameworks and standards that guide coaches in navigating this dynamic environment, stressing the urgency of staying updated.

The conclusion of this chapter marks the beginning of a new era for coaching in corporate innovation. Coaches who rise to the challenge will find themselves not merely as facilitators of change but as architects of transformation. By aligning human potential with technological capabilities, fostering inclusive cultures, and championing ethical leadership, coaches will help organizations confidently navigate complexity and uncertainty.

In the end, the role of the coach is not to provide answers but to enable others to discover their potential. As the world of corporate innovation continues to evolve, this ability to inspire and empower will remain the cornerstone of effective coaching. The future belongs to those who can adapt, collaborate, and innovate—and coaches will be there to guide them every step of the way.

Part V

Conclusion and a Call to Action

Call to Action

This book synthesizes the core themes and insights presented throughout, emphasizing the pivotal role of coaching strategies for corporate innovation, specifically for corporate–startup collaboration in the form of open innovation. This work has explored three critical dimensions: matching innovation, collaborative innovation, and the ecosystem of innovation. Each chapter contributes to and builds upon the previous one for an overall understanding of how corporates can leverage coaching to navigate the complexities of innovation in today's dynamic business environment.

Coaching Strategies for Matching Innovation

The chapters on matching innovation highlight the necessity of aligning leadership with innovative practices. For leading and implementing corporate innovation initiatives, corporates must prioritize selecting leaders with vision and exemplary character. The case studies illustrate that misalignment between a startup's founder and corporate objectives can lead to significant setbacks. Emphasizing the importance of character over technological prowess, we show that corporates should adopt effective coaching strategies that assess value-based leadership qualities.

A systematic approach is crucial for matching innovation with corporate strategies. Establishing a shared vision among stakeholders fosters alignment and drives successful innovation initiatives. Corporates can effectively address challenges and seize growth opportunities by creating an environment where collaboration thrives.

Coaching Strategies for Collaborative Innovation

We deep-dive into the significance of trust and cultural integration between corporate and startups in collaborative innovation. Their successful collaboration depends heavily on establishing a culture that values emotional intelligence and open communication. The case studies presented demonstrate how trust serves as a foundation for effective teamwork, instilling a sense of reassurance and confidence in the collaborative process.

DOI: 10.4324/9781003469155-14

It is tantamount for corporates to come to terms with the fact that cultural clashes impede progress and, in most cases, will lead to failed partnerships. By implementing coaching strategies focused on trust-building, companies can cultivate an environment conducive to collaboration. Emphasizing emotional intelligence showcases its critical role in shaping team dynamics, enabling diverse groups to work together effectively.

Corporate–startup collaboration is about nurturing long-term relationships critical to driving sustainable innovation. By prioritizing collaborative efforts, organizations position themselves to adapt to market changes and leverage external expertise successfully.

Coaching Strategies for the Ecosystem of Innovation

The chapters "Progressive Pivoting" and "An Emergent Role" emphasized the interconnectedness of various stakeholders and the appetite for innovation in driving corporate–startup collaboration forward. Corporates must recognize their place within a broader ecosystem, including startups, investors, educational institutions, and other entities. This ecosystem approach cultivates a continuous learning and adaptation culture in an accelerating technological and disruptive economy.

We analyzed progressive pivoting as an essential strategy for corporates facing evolving market demands. Successful companies have pivots by engaging their teams and leveraging insights from diverse sources. Implementing appropriate coaching strategies plays a vital role in facilitating these transitions, ensuring that employees remain engaged and motivated during periods of change.

Furthermore, we addressed the importance of integrating sustainability into innovation practices. As corporates strive to meet societal expectations and environmental challenges, they must embed sustainable practices into their core strategies. This commitment enhances corporate reputation while driving long-term success.

Final Thoughts and a Call to Action

In this exploration of coaching strategies for corporate innovation, it is evident that the corporate–startup leadership team must adopt a proactive mindset to thrive in today's dynamic landscape. The insights presented in this book provide strategies to cultivate a culture of innovation for their corporate–startup collaboration.

This book serves as a vital resource for leaders, coaches, and innovators aiming to navigate the complexities of corporate innovation successfully.

Through real-world examples, case studies, frameworks, and practical coaching strategies, this book invites readers to reimagine the possibilities of corporate innovation and believe that coaching can unlock unprecedented opportunities for innovation and transformation across industries.

Call to Action

1   Bridging the People-Technology Potentials: Coaching has always been centered around unlocking potential and guiding professional development and growth. Technology will continue to disrupt and reshape the professional landscape. Coaches must embrace new tools and methods to remain relevant and leverage them. The future of coaching lies in the ability to optimize human insight with technological capability, creating an environment where both can thrive symbiotically.

   Coaches must be proactive in integrating technology into their coaching repertoire. This integration is about efficiently utilizing tools and enhancing the coaching experience. For instance, coaches can enrich their work by blending their emotional intelligence with technological insights to provide personalized, data-informed coaching that still maintains the depth of human interaction. This could involve using AI-powered platforms to analyze client data and provide personalized recommendations or virtual reality to create immersive coaching experiences. As an example, coaches using platforms that track behavioral data or performance analytics will be able to guide their clients more efficiently and effectively. The discerning usage of technology helps them interpret the numbers in ways that align with their values and long-term goals. By translating data into actionable insights, coaches bridge the gap between raw information and real-world application. Coaches must remain the interpreters of data, contextualizing it within the client's unique human experience and needs.

2   **Cultivating Lifelong Learning and Adaptability:** Every coach must continuously update their skills and knowledge base as technology advances incessantly. This practice requires an ongoing commitment to learning—not just about emerging tools but also about how these tools can be best applied in various coaching contexts. The successful coach of the future will be one who is equally adept at navigating human emotions as they are at using technology to facilitate progress.

   Coaches should invest in professional development that includes technological literacy and deepening their core coaching skills. They should become proficient in the tools that best serve their clients while also sharpening their emotional intelligence to ensure that the human element remains at the forefront of the coaching process.

3   **Upholding Ethical Standards and Connecting People:** Digitalization and the increasing use of digital tools are the norm in the marketplace. Nevertheless, coaching must remain rooted in ethical responsibility and people-centered. Coaches are to adhere to these principles steadfastly, ensuring that technology does not erode the trust and accountability that coaching requires. Coaches must prioritize transparency, confidentiality, and informed consent when using new technological tools, which are in line with the ethical standards that define their profession.

For instance, as new coaching technologies gather and analyze data, coaches must ensure their clients understand how the data will be used and the potential benefits and risks. Clear boundaries and ethical guidelines ensure that clients feel safe and valued, even in a highly digitalized environment. Coaches have the unique responsibility to preserve the human aspect of coaching, even as technology becomes more integral to their practice.

4   Building Collaboration Between Humans and Technology: The future of coaching depends on the collaboration between human coaches and technological tools. Coaches should see technology as an ally, not a replacement. As new tools emerge, coaches must remain proactive in understanding how to use them in a way that maximizes potential. What this means is that we should utilize technology as a partner in helping clients achieve better results. For example, AI platforms that provide feedback or progress tracking will be able to monitor clients' development over time and ensure that each step aligns with their core values and objectives. Coaches can then offer strategic advice, while technology provides data and insights to guide these decisions. Coaches and technology can create a dynamic, adaptable coaching experience that is more powerful than either could be alone.

5   **Leading by Example in Innovation and Adaptation:** Coaches must not only integrate technology into their practices but also lead by example in adapting to new ways of working. Clients will look to their coaches to navigate the evolving landscape, making it essential for coaches to stay ahead of trends. By embracing technology, coaches demonstrate the power of adaptation and innovation, encouraging their clients to adopt these attitudes in their personal and professional lives.

Coaches who embrace change openly model a growth mindset, inspiring their clients to approach technology and change with curiosity and openness. As organizations increasingly demand agility, coaches can shape leaders who thrive in complex, ever-changing environments.

While technology can serve as a valuable resource in facilitating personal growth and organizational transformation, it is the unique interpersonal skills of the coach that significantly contribute to meaningful coaching outcomes. Coaches who embrace this paradigm will not only ensure their continued relevance in a changing landscape but will also play a crucial role in shaping future leadership and organizational development. Coaches can enhance the coaching experience, ultimately fostering a more impactful and transformative journey for their clients, by effectively integrating their expertise with technological advancements.

Coaches are always proactive and forward-looking. The call to action serves as a gentle nudge as we embrace and fully leverage technology and channel it to coaching strategies for corporate innovation.

References

Adner, R. (2006). Match your innovation strategy to your innovation ecosystem. *Harvard Business Review*, 84(4), 98–107.

Agarwal, R. (2021). *Scaling fast, scaling smart: The OYO story.* HarperCollins.

Allaho, R., & van Nieuwerburgh, C. (2017). *Coaching in Islamic culture: The principles and practice of Ershad.* Routledge. doi:10.4324/9780429473043

Aulet, B. (2024). *Disciplined entrepreneurship: 24 steps to a successful startup.* Wiley.

Ayoob, S., Shokouhyar, S., & Ahmadi, S. (2022). How digital startups use competitive intelligence to pivot. *Journal of Business Research*, 145, 1–12. doi:10.1016/j.jbusres.2022.05.016

Bao, B., & Lin, X. (2019a). Startup leadership and sustainability in innovation ecosystems. *Journal of Business Research*, 103, 312–324.

Bao, Y., & Lin, X. (2019b). The rise and fall of Ofo: Lessons for startups in hyper-competitive markets. *Journal of Business Strategy*, 40(2),34–45.

Bass, B. M. (1990). From transactional to transformational leadership: Learning to share the vision. *Organizational Dynamics*, 18 (3),19–31.

Bennett, N., & Lemoine, G. J. (2014). What VUCA really means for you. *Harvard Business Review*, 92(1/2), 27.

Bennis, W. (2009). *On becoming a leader.* Basic Books.

Boyatzis, R. (2008). *The emotionally intelligent leader: Developing and sustaining EI in leadership.* Harvard Business Press.

Boyatzis, R., & McKee, A. (2005). *Resonant leadership: Renewing yourself and connecting with others through mindfulness, hope, and compassion.* Harvard Business Review Press.

Bradberry, T., & Greaves, J. (2009). *Emotional intelligence 2.0.* TalentSmart.

Bridoux, F., & Stoelhorst, J. W.(2016).Stakeholder relationships and social welfare: A behavioral theory of contributions to joint value creation. *Academy of Management Review*, 41(2), 229–251. https://doi.org/10.5465/amr.2013.0475

Brown, B. (2018). *Dare to lead: Brave work. Tough conversations. Whole hearts.* Random House.

Built In. (2024). *Optimizing your corporate-startup collaboration.* Retrieved from https://builtin.com.

Burnell, D., Stevenson, R., & Fisher, G. (2023). Early-stage business model experimentation and pivoting. *Journal of Business Venturing*, 38(2), 106024. doi:10.1016/j.jbusvent.2023.106024.

Cameron, K. S., & Quinn, R. E. (2011). *Diagnosing and changing organizational culture: Based on the competing values framework* (3rd ed.). Jossey-Bass.

Carreyrou, J. (2018). *Bad blood: Secrets and lies in a Silicon Valley startup*. Alfred A. Knopf.

Carton, A. M., Murphy, C., & Clark, J. R. (2014b). A (blurry) vision of the future: How leader rhetoric about ultimate goals influences performance. *Academy of Management Journal*, 57(6),1544–1570.

Carton, A. M., Murphy, C., & Pruett, M. (2014a). The role of vision in organizational performance: A review and future directions. *Journal of Management*, 40 (5),1240–1266.

Chen, J., & Chang, K. (2018). An investigation into the business model of bike-sharing: The case of Ofo in China. *Transportation Research Part A: Policy and Practice*, 111, 335–347.

Chen, X., & Chang, J. (2018). Bike-sharing battles: The case of Ofo and Mobike in China. *Harvard Business Review*. Retrieved from https://hbr.org/2018/06/bike-sha ring-battles.

Cherniss, C. (2001). Emotional intelligence and organizational effectiveness. In C. Cherniss & D. Goleman (Eds.), *The emotionally intelligent workplace* (pp. 3–26). Jossey-Bass.

Chesbrough, H. W. (2003). *Open innovation: The new imperative for creating and profiting from technology*. Harvard Business School Press.

Chesbrough, H. W. (2011). *Open services innovation: Rethinking your business to grow and compete in a new era*. Jossey-Bass.

Chin, S. (2021). *Super apps: The battle for Southeast Asia*. Penguin.

Christensen, C. M. (2016). *The innovator's dilemma: When new technologies cause great firms to fail*. Harvard Business Review Press.

Christensen, C. M., & Raynor, M. E.(2013).*The innovator's solution: Creating and sustaining successful growth*. Harvard Business Review Press.

Christensen, C. M., Raynor, M. E., & McDonald, R. (2015). *The innovator's dilemma: When new technologies cause great firms to fail*. Harvard Business Review Press.

Christensen, C. M., Bartman, T., & van Bever, D. (2016). The hard truth about business model innovation. *Harvard Business Review*.

Ciulla, J. B. (2004a). *The ethics of leadership*. Routledge.

Ciulla, J. B. (2004b). *Ethics, the heart of leadership*. Praeger.

Clark, D. (2016). *Alibaba: The house that Jack Ma built*. Ecco Press.

Clifton, D. O., Anderson, E., & Schreiner, L. A. (2006a). *CliftonStrengths*. Gallup Press.

Clifton, D. O., Anderson, E., & Schreiner, L. A. (2006b). *StrengthsQuest: Discover and develop your strengths in academics, career, and beyond*. Gallup Press.

Clutterbuck, D. (2010). *Coaching the team at work*. Nicholas Brealey Publishing.

Clutterbuck, D. (2013). *Coaching the team at work* (2nd ed.). Nicholas Brealey Publishing.

Clutterbuck, D. (2020). *Coaching the team at work: The definitive guide to team coaching*. Nicholas Brealey Publishing.

Clutterbuck, D., & Megginson, D. (2004). *Techniques for coaching and mentoring*. Gower Publishing.

Clutterbuck, D., Megginson, D., &Bajer, A. (2016). *Building and sustaining a coaching culture: A developmental approach*. CIPD Publishing.

Clutterbuck, D., Megginson, D., & David, M. (Eds.). (2013). *Beyond goals: Effective strategies for coaching and mentoring*. Routledge.

CoachHub. (2023). *Democratizing leadership: The impact of AI in coaching*. CoachHub Research Report.

Collins, J. C., & Porras, J. I. (1996). *Built to last: Successful habits of visionary companies*. HarperBusiness.

Collins, J. (2001). *Good to great: Why some companies make the leap and others don't*. HarperCollins.

Collins, J., & Porras, J. I. (1996). Building your company's vision. *Harvard Business Review*, 74(5),65–77.

Cooper, R. G. (2018). *Winning at new products: Creating value through innovation* (5th ed.). Basic Books.

Corrie, S.(2024).What's the story? The contribution of formulation to coaching practice in complex times. *The Coaching Psychologist*, 20(1), 71–80.

Corrie, S., & Kovacs, L. (2019). *Formulation in action: Applying psychological theory to coaching practice*. Karnac Books.

Corrie, S., & Kovacs, L. (2017). The art of formulation in coaching psychology: A developmental perspective. *The Coaching Psychologist*, 13(1), 26–33.

Corrie, S., & Lane, D. A. (2010). Constructing stories in coaching: Re-authoring lives in transition. *International Coaching Psychology Review*, 5(1), 62–70.

Costa, A. C., Passos, A. M., & Bakker, A. B. (2001). Trust within teams: The relation with performance effectiveness. *European Journal of Work and Organizational Psychology*, 10(3),227–245. doi:10.1080/13594320143000654.

Covey, S. M. R. (2006). *The speed of trust: The one thing that changes everything*. Free Press.

Covey, S. R. (2004a). *The 7 habits of highly effective people: Powerful lessons in personal change*. Free Press.

Covey, S. R. (2004b). *The 8th habit: From effectiveness to greatness*. Free Press.

Dannar, P. (2016). If you want creativity in your organizations, seek out the introvert. *Journal of Leadership Studies*, 10(1),40–41. doi:10.1002/jls.21438

Deloitte. (2021). Innovation in the era of disruption: A report on the state of innovation in the US.

Deming, W. E. (2000). *Out of the crisis*. MIT Press.

Denison, D. R., & Mishra, A. K. (1995). Toward a theory of organizational culture and effectiveness. *Organization Science*, 6(2),204–223.

Djordjevic, J. (2021a). The importance of vision in strategic management. *Journal of Strategic Leadership*, 9(2),15–29.

Djordjevic, M. (2021b). The impact of vision on organizational performance: A systematic review. *International Journal of Management Reviews*, 23 (1),54–75.

Drake, D. B. (2011). *Narrative coaching: The definitive guide to bringing new stories to life*. CNC Press.

Dweck, C. S. (2006). *Mindset: The new psychology of success*. Random House.

DK. (2024). *Simply AI: Facts made fast*. DK Publishing.

Doran, G. T. (1981). There's a S.M.A.R.T. way to write management's goals and objectives. *Management Review*, 70(11),35–36.

Druskat, V. U., & Wolff, S. B. (2001). Building the emotional intelligence of groups. *Harvard Business Review*, 79(3),81–90.

Duarte, F.(2024).ChatGPT 2024 retrospective: Innovation that transformed the year. *Roberto Dias Duarte Blog*, December 31. https://www.robertodiasduarte.com.br/en/retrospectiva-chatgpt-2024-inovacao-que-transformou-o-ano/

Duckworth, A. (2016). *Grit: The power of passion and perseverance.* Scribner.

Dweck, C. S. (2006). *Mindset: The new psychology of success.* Random House.

Easton, C., & Steyn, R. (2023). Millennial leaders and leadership styles displayed in the workplace. *South African Journal of Business Management, 54*(1), a3139. doi:10.4102/sajbm.v54i1.3139.

Edmondson, A. C. (1999a). Psychological safety and learning behavior in work teams. *Administrative Science Quarterly,* 44(2),350–383.

Edmondson, A. C. (1999b). *The fearless organization: Creating psychological safety in the workplace for learning, innovation and growth.* Wiley.

Edmondson, A. C. (2018). *The fearless organization: Creating psychological safety in the workplace for learning, innovation, and growth.* Wiley.

Edmondson, A. C., Bohmer, R. M. J., & Pisano, G. P. (2001). Disrupted routines: Team learning and new technology implementation in hospitals. *Administrative Science Quarterly,* 46(4),685–718. doi:10.2307/3094826

European Mentoring and Coaching Council (EMCC). (n.d.). *Coaching supervision.* Retrieved November 10, 2024, from https://www.emccglobal.org/coaching-supervision/.

Falvo, R., Hagahmed, A., & Chan, J. (2023a). Design thinking in startups: A framework for innovation. *Harvard Business Review.*

Falvo, T., Hagahmed, W., & Chan, E. (2023b). Understanding the power of design thinking: Empathy as a driving force. *Journal of Design and Innovation,* 18(1),45–59.

Fan, L. (2017). Trust in business ecosystems: The Alibaba model. *Journal of Business Strategy,* 38(5),140–149.

Feld, Brad. (2024). In B. Aulet, *Disciplined entrepreneurship: 24 steps to a successful startup* (p. 3). Wiley.

Finkelstein, S., Hambrick, D. C., & Cannella, A. A. (2009). *Strategic leadership: Theory and research on executives, top management teams, and boards.* Oxford University Press.

Flaherty, J. (2010). *Coaching: Evoking excellence in others.* Elsevier.

Flechas Chaparro, X. A., & de Vasconcelos Gomes, L. A. (2021). Pivot decisions in startups: A systematic literature review. *International Journal of Entrepreneurial Behavior & Research,* 27(4),884–910. doi:10.1108/IJEBR-12-2019-0699.

Forbes. (2020, January 30). *Nubank's David Vélez: The bank slayer.* Retrieved from https://www.forbes.com.

Forbes. (2020). *NuBank's leadership and growth.* Retrieved from https://www.forbes.com.

Forbes. (2021). *Adaptation to market changes.* Retrieved from https://www.forbes.com/sites/forbescoachescouncil/2021/01/17/adaptation-to-market-changes/?sh=1d5e7f7a7f6a.

Forbes. (2020). *Integrity and its impact on business success.* Retrieved from https://www.forbes.com/sites/forbescoachescouncil/2020/01/17/integrity-and-its-impact-on-business-success/?sh=1d5e7f7a7f6a.

Fouracres, A. J. S., & van Nieuwerburgh, C. (2020). The lived experience of self-identifying character strengths through coaching: An interpretative phenomenological analysis. *International Journal of Evidence-Based Coaching and Mentoring,* 18 (1),43–56. doi:10.24384/e0jp-9m61

Gans, J., Stern, S., & Wu, J. (2019). The strategy of startups. *Harvard Business Review.*

Gassmann, O., Enkel, E., & Chesbrough, H. (2010). The future of open innovation. *R&D Management,* 40(3),213–221.

Gino, F., & Staats, B. R. (2015). Why organizations don't learn. *Harvard Business Review,* 93(2),8–14.

Goleman, D. (1995). *Emotional intelligence: Why it can matter more than IQ*. Bantam Books.

Goleman, D. (1998). *Working with emotional intelligence*. Bantam Books.

Goleman, D. (1998). What makes a leader? *Harvard Business Review*, 76(6),93–102.

Goleman, D. (2000). Leadership that gets results. *Harvard Business Review*, 78(2),78–90.

Goleman, D., Boyatzis, R., & McKee, A. (2002). *Primal leadership: Realizing the power of emotional intelligence*. Harvard Business School Press.

Gompers, P., & Lerner, J. (2013). *The venture capital cycle*. MIT Press.

Han, S. (2022). What is design thinking & why is it important? *Harvard Business School Blog*. Retrieved from https://www.hbs.edu.

Harvard Business Review. (2016). *Coachability in founders*. Retrieved from https://hbr.org/2016/07/coachability-in-founders.

Harvard Business Review. (2015). *The importance of emotional intelligence in leadership*. Retrieved from https://hbr.org/2015/06/the-importance-of-emotional-intelligence-in-leadership.

Hawkins, P. (2012). *Creating a coaching culture: Developing a coaching strategy for your organization*. McGraw-Hill.

Heifetz, R. A., & Linsky, M. (2002). *Leadership on the line: Staying alive through the dangers of leading*. Harvard Business Review Press.

Hitt, M. A., Ireland, R. D., & Hoskisson, R. E. (2017). *Strategic management: Competitiveness and globalization* (12th ed.). Cengage Learning.

Hofstede, G. (2001). *Culture's consequences: Comparing values, behaviors, institutions, and organizations across nations* (2nd ed.). Sage Publications.

Hogan, R., & Kaiser, R. B. (2005). What we know about leadership. *Review of General Psychology*, 9 (2),169–180.

Hollywood, J., Kavanagh, M., & Eastman, A. (2016). Holistic mentoring and coaching to sustain organisational change and innovation. *International Journal of Evidence Based Coaching and Mentoring*, 12 (2),33–47.

Hollywood, K. G., Blaess, D. A., Santin, C., & Bloom, L. (2016). Holistic mentoring and coaching to sustain organizational change and innovation. *Creighton Journal of Interdisciplinary Leadership*, 2(1),32–46.

Hubert, B. (2020). Move seat design for Airbus. *Design Journal*, 34(3),52–58.

Hughes, J. (2021). Nike and RTFKT: How a collaboration is defining the future of digital fashion. *Harvard Business Review*. Retrieved from https://hbr.org/2021/11/nike-rtfkt-collaboration.

Humans of Globe. (n.d.). *Leaders must pivot or perish: Agility and innovation*. Retrieved from https://humansofglobe.com/leaders-pivot-or-perish-agility-and-innovation/.

International Coaching Federation (ICF). (n.d.). *Coaching supervision*. Retrieved November 10, 2024, from https://coachingfederation.org/credentials-and-standards/coaching-supervision.

Isaacson, W. (2011). *Steve Jobs*. Simon & Schuster.

Jones, T. (2020). Ergonomics and its role in the future of airline seating. *Journal of Applied Ergonomics*, 45(1),23–28.

Kale, P., Singh, H., & Perlmutter, H. (2000). Learning and protection of proprietary assets in strategic alliances: Building relational capital. *Strategic Management Journal*, 21 (3),217–237.

Kasasa. (2021, July 6). Boomers, gen X, gen Y, gen Z, and gen A explained. *Kasasa Exchange.* Retrieved November 10, 2024, from https://offer.kasasa.com/exchange/a rticles/generations/gen-x-gen-y-gen-z.

Kasneci, E., Sessler, K., Küchemann, S., Bannert, M., Dementieva, D., Fischer, F., et al. (2023). ChatGPT for good? On opportunities and challenges of large language models for education. *Learning and Individual Differences*, 103, 102274. doi:10.1016/ j.lindif.2023.102274.

Kawasaki, G. (2004). *The art of the start: The time-tested, battle-hardened guide for anyone starting anything.* Portfolio.

Kerr, W. R., Nanda, R., & Rhodes-Kropf, M. (2014). Entrepreneurial finance: Venture capital, deal structure, and valuation. *Harvard Business School.*

Kiron, D., Kruschwitz, N., Haanaes, K., Reeves, M., & Goh, E. (2013). The innova- tion bottom line. *MIT Sloan Management Review*, 54(2),69–78.

Korn Ferry. (2014). *Leadership architect competency sort cards.* Korn Ferry Institute.

Kotter, J. P. (2012). *Leading change.* Harvard Business Review Press.

Kouzes, J. M., & Posner, B. Z. (2012). *The leadership challenge: How to make extraordinary things happen in organizations.* Jossey-Bass.

Kouzes, J. M., & Posner, B. Z. (2017). *The leadership challenge: How to make extraordinary things happen in organizations (6th ed.).* Jossey-Bass.

Kovacs, L. (2016). Coaching psychology and its relevance to organisational practice. *Coaching Psychology International*, 9(2), 8–15.

Kraaijenbrink, J. (2018). What does VUCA really mean? *Forbes.* https://www.forbes.com/ sites/jeroenkraaijenbrink/2018/01/16/what-does-vuca-really-mean/?sh=39a446a12f11.

Lane, D. A., & Corrie, S. (2009). Does coaching psychology need the concept of for- mulation? *International Coaching Psychology Review*, 4(2),145–155.

Lane, D. A., Corrie, S., & Kovacs, L. (2025). *A guide to Formulation in Coaching.* Routledge.

Lee, G. K., & Yoo, Y. (2010). How Samsung became a design powerhouse. *Harvard Business Review*, 88(6),136–142.

Lee, K., & Yoo, Y. (2010). Samsung Electronics: Managing innovations in an eco- nomic downturn. *Innovation: Management, Policy & Practice*, 12 (1),134–144.

Lee, S., & Yong, I. (2019). *Department of start up: Why every Fortune 500 should have one.* BEP.

Lencioni, P. (2002). *The five dysfunctions of a team: A leadership fable.* Jossey-Bass.

Lev-Ram, M. (2020, October 21). The rise and fall of Quibi. *Fortune.* Retrieved from https://fortune.com/2020/10/21/quibi-what-went-wrong-streaming/.

Liker, J. K. (2004). *The Toyota way: 14 management principles from the world's greatest manufacturer.* McGraw-Hill.

Ma, J. (2016). *Alibaba: Lessons in trust and leadership.* Ecco Press.

Macmillan Publishers. (n.d.). *The rise and fall of Theranos.* Retrieved from https:// www.panmacmillan.com/blogs/literary/theranos-elizabeth-holmes-john-carreyrou.

Mayer, R. C., Davis, J. H., & Schoorman, F. D. (1995). An integrative model of organizational trust. *Academy of Management Review*, 20(3),709–734.

Medyanik, K. K. (2016). A holistic, qualitative case study regarding the leadership traits and styles of the millennial generation (Doctoral dissertation, Northcentral University).

Mishe, P. (2000a). Six principles of an effective vision statement. *Journal of Organisa- tional Studies*, 17(4),22–30.

Mishe, S. (2000b). The essential qualities of an effective vision: An empirical study in organizational settings. *Journal of Business Research*, 47 (3),237–248.

Nahapiet, J., & Ghoshal, S. (1998). Social capital, intellectual capital, and the organizational advantage. *Academy of Management Review*, 23(2),242–266.

Nanus, B. (1992). *Visionary leadership: creating a compelling sense of direction for your organization.* Jossey-Bass.

Natarajan, K. (2020). *Digital disruption and corporate innovation: Creating value in a changing world.* Elsevier.

Neenan, M., & Palmer, S. (2001). Cognitive behavioural coaching. *The Psychologist*, 14 (2),63–66.

Northouse, P. G. (2018). *Leadership: Theory and practice* (8th ed.). Sage Publications.

Nutt, P., & Backoff, R. W. (1997). Transforming organisations with strategic vision. *Strategic Management Journal*, 18(3),153–171.

Nutt, P. C., & Backoff, R. W. (1997). The role of vision in organizational change: A study of the United States Navy's transition to the all-volunteer force. *Journal of Organizational Change Management*, 10 (2),161–177.

O'Neill, M. B. (2007). *Executive coaching with backbone and heart: A systems approach to engaging leaders with their challenges.* Jossey-Bass.

O'Reilly, C. A., & Tushman, M. L. (2016). *Lead and disrupt: How to solve the innovator's dilemma.* Stanford Business Books.

Patel, B., & van Nieuwerburgh, C. (2022). Exploring the experience of coaches in an international non-profit organisation using a values-based coaching framework. *International Journal of Evidence Based Coaching and Mentoring*, 20 (2), 99–114. doi 10.24384/nf8q-7d23

Peeters, P., Higham, J., Kutzner, D., & Cohen, S. (2019). Sustainable aviation futures: Technical and policy perspectives. *Journal of Transport Geography*, 74, 376–388.

Pentland, A. (2012). The new science of building great teams. *Harvard Business Review*, 90(4),60–70.

Peters, L. (2018). Challenges in retail collaborations: Insights from the Target-Chef'd partnership. *Retail Industry Journal*.

Peterson, C., & Seligman, M. E. P. (2004). *Character strengths and virtues: A handbook and classification.* American Psychological Association; Oxford University Press.

Pisano, G. P.(2019).The hard truth about innovative cultures. *Harvard Business Review*, 97(1), 62–71. https://hbr.org/2019/01/the-hard-truth-about-innovative-cultures.

Polman, P. (2016). *Unilever's sustainable living plan: Progress report.* Unilever.

Puranam, P., Alexy, O., & Reitzig, M. (2014). What's "new" about new forms of organizing? *Academy of Management Review*, 39(2),162–180.

PwC. (2017). Innovation benchmark report: Global insights on innovation.

Radziwon, A., Chesbrough, H., Vanhaverbeke, W., & West, J. (2023). The future of open innovation. In *The Oxford Handbook of Open Innovation.* Oxford University Press.

Ransford, K. (2018). *The rise and fall of Chef'd: Lessons from the meal kit industry.* Chef'd.

Reeves, M., & Deimler, M. (2011). Adaptability: The new competitive advantage. *Harvard Business Review*, 89(7–8),134–141.

Reuters. (2018, October 8). *Tencent buys stake in Brazil's Nubank in $200 million deal.* Retrieved from https://www.reuters.com.

Ries, E. (2011). *The lean startup: How today's entrepreneurs use continuous innovation to create radically successful businesses.* Crown Business.

Rigby, D. K., Sutherland, J., & Takeuchi, H. (2016). Embracing agile. *Harvard Business Review, 94*(5),40–48.

Roberts, E. B., & Eesley, C. E. (2009). Entrepreneurial impact: The role of MIT. *Foundations and Trends® in Entrepreneurship,* 7(1–2),1–149.

Sala, P. K., Philbin, S. P., & Barikzai, S. (2022). A qualitative research study of the tech startup journey through entrepreneurial pivoting. *International Journal of Entrepreneurial Behavior & Research,* 28(4),1050–1074. doi:10.1108/IJEBR-07-2021-0528

Salovey, P., & Mayer, J. D. (1990). Emotional intelligence. *Imagination, Cognition, and Personality,* 9(3),185–211.

Samsung Electronics. (2017). *Annual report 2017.* Retrieved from Samsung website.

Samsung NEXT. (2020). *Innovation and investment in startups.* Retrieved from Samsung NEXT website.

Sarhan, F., & Ahmed, S. (2020). *Corporate innovation and market adaptation in the MENA region.* Palgrave McMillan.

Schaal, D. (2017). Alibaba buys controlling stake in Southeast Asia's Lazada. *Skift.*

Schein, E. H. (2004). *Organizational culture and leadership.* Jossey-Bass.

Schein, E. H. (2010). *Organizational culture and leadership* (4th ed.). Jossey-Bass.

Schein, E. H. (2016). *Organizational culture and leadership* (5th ed.). Wiley.

Schwartz, P. (1991). *The art of the long view: Planning for the future in an uncertain world.* Doubleday.

Schwartz, S. H. (1992). Universals in the content and structure of values: Theoretical advances and empirical tests in 20 countries. *Advances in Experimental Social Psychology,* 25, 1–65. doi:10.1016/S0065-2601(08)60281–60286

Schwartz, S. H. (2012). An overview of the Schwartz theory of basic values. *Online Readings in Psychology and Culture,* 2(1),1–20. doi:10.9707/2307-0919.1116

Senge, P. M. (1990). *The fifth discipline: The art and practice of the learning organization.* Doubleday/Currency.

Shepherd, D. A., & DeTienne, D. R. (2005). Prior knowledge, potential financial rewards, and the decision to start a business. *Entrepreneurship Theory and Practice, 29*(1),91–112.

Sherman, A. (2020, October 21). Quibi is shutting down just six months after going live. *CNBC.* Retrieved from https://www.cnbc.com/2020/10/21/quibi-is-shutting-down.html.

Sherman, L. (2020, October 21). Katzenberg and Whitman shutter Quibi. *The Hollywood Reporter.*

Sinek, S. (2009). *Start with why: How great leaders inspire everyone to take action.* Portfolio/Penguin.

Skok, D. (2024). Transformational leadership in action. *Leadership Quarterly,* 35 (2),29–48.

Sohaib, M., Soomro, T. R., Tahir, A., & Alvi, A. (2017). An analysis of major pivots of software startups. *Journal of Systems and Software,* 126, 1–12. doi:10.1016/j.jss.2016.10.001.

Spangler, T. (2020, October 22). Why Quibi crashed and burned in less than seven months. *Variety.* Retrieved from https://variety.com/2020/digital/news/quibi-failure-shutdown-1234813765/.

Stanford Graduate School of Business. (2021). David Vélez, MBA '12. Retrieved from https://www.gsb.stanford.edu/insights/david-velez-position-yourself-scarcity-not-oversupply

StartUs Insights. (n.d.). *Full guide to corporate open innovation: Unlock growth & visibility.* Retrieved from https://www.startus-insights.com/innovators-guide/data-driven-open-innovation/.

Stober, D. R., & Grant, A. M. (2006). *Evidence-based coaching handbook: Putting best practices to work for your clients.* Wiley.

Stone, B. (2017). *The everything store: Jeff Bezos and the age of Amazon.* Little, Brown and Company.

Stringham, E. M., Miller, J. K., & Clark, J. R. (2015). Overcoming barriers to entry in an established industry: Tesla Motors. *California Management Review,* 57(4),85–103.

Su, X., Wang, T., & Li, J. (2004). A systems perspective on vision in organisational strategy. *Systems Research and Behavioural Science,* 21(5),381–390.

Su, Z., Zhang, X., & Wang, Y. (2004). Organizational vision and its impact on performance: Evidence from Chinese companies. *Management Decision,* 42 (8),1015–1029.

Sun, L., & Zhang, H. (2020). Urban mobility innovations and their discontents: The case of Ofo in China. *Transportation Research Part A: Policy and Practice,* 132, 256–269.

Tan, A. (2021). *Building Southeast Asia's super-app: Grab's journey to market dominance.* Routledge.

Taneja, S., Pryor, M. G., & Humphreys, J. H. (2019). *Strategic management: A dynamic view.* Routledge.

Tannenbaum, S. I., Beard, R. L., & Salas, E. (1992). Team building and its influence on team effectiveness: An examination of conceptual and empirical developments. In K. Kelley (Ed.), *Issues, theory, and research in industrial/organizational psychology* (pp. 117–153). Elsevier Science.

Target Corporation. (2018). Target's partnerships and collaborations: A path to grocery innovation.

Terblanche, N., Molyn, J., de Haan, E., & Nilsson, V. O. (2022). Comparing artificial intelligence and human coaching goal attainment efficacy. *PLOS ONE,* 17(6), e0270255. doi:10.1371/journal.pone.0270255

Thompson, D. (2016). How GM and Lyft are teaming up to build the future of transportation. *The Atlantic.* Retrieved from https://www.theatlantic.com/technology/archive/2016/01/gm-lyft-partnership/431037/.

TechCrunch. (2019, September 20). *Nubank raises $400M.* Retrieved from https://techcrunch.com.

Tian, L., Logendran, M., & Mariappan, R. (2023). Communication skills and persuasion: A quantitative evaluation. *Journal of Organisational Behaviour,* 44(2),119–134.

Tidd, J., & Bessant, J. (2018). *Managing innovation: Integrating technological, market, and organizational change* (6th ed.). John Wiley & Sons.

Toon, N. (2024). *How AI thinks: How we built it, how it can help us, and how we can control it.* Torva, an imprint of Transworld, a division of Penguin Random House.

Valdez-Juárez, L. E., & Castillo-Vergara, M. (2021). Technological capabilities, open innovation, and eco-innovation: Dynamic capabilities to increase corporate performance of SMEs. *Journal of Open Innovation: Technology, Market, and Complexity,* 7(1), 8. doi:10.3390/joitmc7010008.

Vaswani, A., Shazeer, N., Parmar, N., Uszkoreit, J., Jones, L., Gomez, A. N., Kaiser, Ł., & Polosukhin, I. (2017). Attention is all you need. *Proceedings of the 31st International Conference on Neural Information Processing Systems (NIPS 2017),* 30, 5998–6008.

Vlessing, E. (2020, October 21). Quibi founders Jeffrey Katzenberg, Meg Whitman announce shutdown. *The Hollywood Reporter.* Retrieved from https://www.hollywoodreporter.com/business/digital/quibi-shutting-down-4079821/.

Weber, R. A., & Camerer, C. F. (2003). Cultural conflict and merger failure: An experimental approach. *Management Science,* 49(4),400–415.

Weiblen, T., & Chesbrough, H. W. (2015). Engaging with startups to enhance corporate innovation. *California Management Review*, 57(2),66–90.

West, J., & Bogers, M. (2014). Leveraging external sources of innovation: A review of research on open innovation. *Journal of Product Innovation Management*, 31 (4),814–831.

Westerman, G., Bonnet, D., & McAfee, A. (2014). *Leading digital: Turning technology into business transformation*. Harvard Business Review Press.

Whitmore, J. (2017). *Coaching for performance: The principles and practice of coaching and leadership* (5th ed.). Nicholas Brealey Publishing.

Wiggers, K., Corrall, C., & Stringer, A. (2024, November 1). ChatGPT: Everything you need to know about the AI chatbot. *TechCrunch*. Retrieved November 10, 2024, from https://techcrunch.com/2024/11/01/chatgpt-everything-to-know-about-the-ai-chatbot/.

Wikipedia. (n.d.). *Deep Blue (chess computer)*. In Wikipedia. Retrieved November 10, 2024, from https://en.wikipedia.org/wiki/Deep_Blue_(chess_computer).

Wikipedia contributors. (2024, November 16). ChatGPT. *Wikipedia, The Free Encyclopedia*. Retrieved November 10, 2024, from https://en.wikipedia.org/wiki/ChatGPT.

Wilson, A. (2021). Digital transformations in airline customer service: The rise of smart technology. *International Journal of Aviation Management*, 12(2),85–90.

Wilson, M. (2018). Target's journey in the grocery sector: An analysis of strategic partnerships. *Strategic Retail Management Journal*.

World Economic Forum. (2023). *Top 10 emerging technologies 2023*.

Wu, X. (2020). Globalization and trust: The role of Alibaba in cross-border collaborations. *International Journal of Business*, 25(4),195–210.

Yoffie, D. B., & Rossano, G. (2018). Apple Inc. in 2018. *Harvard Business School Case 9–717–419*.

*Zak, P. J.(*2017). *The trust factor: The science of creating high-performance companies*. AMACOM.

Zhou, L., & Wu, J. (2019). Research on the business model of Ofo based on the perspective of stakeholders. *Open Journal of Business and Management*, 7(1),223–232.

Index

technical dialogue 129
technological innovation 27
technology-centric approach 28
Terblanche, N. 132–134
Tesla, Inc. 7
Theranos 29, 45
Tian, L. 54, 55
Tidd, J.: *Managing Innovation: Integrating Technological, Market, and Organizational Change* 4
Toon, Nigel: *How AI Thinks: How We Built It, How It Can Help Us, and How We Can Control It* 131
transformational coaching 97
transformational technology 131
trust: before collaboration 23; issues and operational misalignment 88; legacy of 93; and psychological safety 20; and relationship building 9
trust-building: exercises 86, 101; structured road map for 86
Tushman, M. L.: *Lead and Disrupt: How to Solve the Innovator's Dilemma* 4

values-alignment workshops 40, 43
values-based coaching 123, 136–137
Values in Action Inventory of Strengths Survey (VIA-IS) 136

van Nieuwerburgh, C. 137
Vaswani, A. 62
Vélez, David 29, 32, 33
VIA Character Strengths Survey 40
visions 49–50; as act of leadership 53–55; alignment 48; commitment to 55–56; development 48; development in corporate *versus* startups 51–52; dual components of 47–48; and goals, aligning 38; innovation is inherent in startup's 52–53; loyalty 48; in startups 48; as strategic guidance 47
vision-setting process 52
vivid description 50
volatile, uncertain, complex, and ambiguous (VUCA): economy 3; environment 121

Weber, R. A. 72
Wei, Dai 29
well-conceived vision 49
West, J. 16
Whitman, Meg 30
Wible, Edward 32
World Economic Forum 3

Zak, Paul 128

For Product Safety Concerns and Information please contact our EU
representative GPSR@taylorandfrancis.com
Taylor & Francis Verlag GmbH, Kaufingerstraße 24, 80331 München, Germany

www.ingramcontent.com/pod-product-compliance
Lightning Source LLC
Chambersburg PA
CBHW052008270326
41929CB00015B/2842